# SWAMI VIVEKANANDA
## THE MONK AND THE REFORMER

# SWAMI VIVEKANANDA

WHAT SWAMI VIVEKANANDA DID
WHAT SWAMI VIVEKANANDA SAID

# THE MONK AND THE REFORMER

Edited by Anu Kumar

First published in 2014 by Hachette India
(Registered name: Hachette Book Publishing India Pvt. Ltd)
An Hachette UK company
www.hachetteindia.com

SRD

Many historical place names have been retained in this book as many places and
regions do not correspond directly or exactly to regions or places now.

ISBN 978-93-5009-825-7

Hachette Book Publishing India Pvt. Ltd,
4th & 5th Floors, Corporate Centre,
Plot No. 94, Sector 44, Gurgaon 122003, India

Typeset in Goudy Old Style BT 10.5/13.5
By Eleven Arts, New Delhi

Printed and bound in India by
Manipal Technologies Limited, Manipal

MIX
Paper | Supporting
responsible forestry
FSC™ C043100

# Contents

'Arise! Awake! And stop not until the goal is reached.'
—Swami Vivekananda

# Early Lessons

**S**wami Vivekananda was born amid political, social and cultural turmoil, and perhaps like with many great men, this tumult shaped him into who he became.

He was born as Narendranath Dutta in 1863 in the city of Calcutta (now Kolkata). It was then the foremost city in British-ruled India. A century and more after the British established a strong presence in Bengal with the East India Company (EIC) assuming control of the province in 1757, this period witnessed many changes. As the British Crown took over the EIC-ruled provinces, more and more Indians were involved with government. Six years had also elapsed since the First Indian War of Independence had broken out in 1857. It was in Barrackpore in north Calcutta that the sepoy Mangal Pandey was hanged for having fired at senior officers, and it set off a chain of events that culminated up north and all across the United Provinces and Central Provinces (now Uttar Pradesh and Madhya Pradesh).

Though the uprising was suppressed, the British knew it was time for transformations. Among these was the formation of the Imperial Civil Service (ICS), officers who were recruited by an elaborate system to administer India. Joining the ICS was coveted by many but till the 1920s, the number of Indians who could join was restricted. Simultaneously, the railways were introduced and expanded, and there were changes in the education system. For example, the universities of Calcutta, Bombay (now Mumbai) and Madras (now Chennai) were all set up in the 1850s, and in the colleges, subjects such as western philosophy, logic and systems of thought were introduced. Education in English began to be imparted in more institutions and schools than before, even those set up by Indians, as the latter realized that this afforded more opportunities for jobs. At the same time, as the number of Indians, especially those in the Presidencies of Bengal, Bombay and Madras, rose among the educated, they began to question British rule. They also became more aware of the ills and problems that plagued their own society.

Calcutta, which had been the centre of the EIC's activities, remained the chief city. There were many who had come to make their fortunes in this city, and among them were Vivekananda's forebears. Originally from Burdwan, to the west of Calcutta, they moved to Govindapur, a village that would later be included in Calcutta, along with others. Narendranath's great-grandfather, Rammohan Dutta, worked for a managing agency, a firm that dabbled in commerce and business while being closely associated with the EIC.

They lived on Shimla Road, a prosperous area, known for its silk-cotton trees that bore fragrant red-white flowers from January to March. It was the tree that gave the road its name (now it has been rechristened Gour Mohan Mukherjee Lane). The area was then a laid-back colony, with spacious houses located in well-tended lawns. His father and grandfather had been prominent lawyers, and the family's fortunes in land had also been built up over generations by dint of merit and sheer hard work.

The house the Duttas lived in was impressive; it had two storeys, and a courtyard that separated the inner chambers from the front rooms that doubled up as offices. There was always, in Narendranath's childhood, an officious-looking *durban* or guard at the main door.

Narendranath was born to Vishwanath Dutta and Bhuvaneshwari Devi on Monday, 12 January 1863. It was the day observed as Makar Sankranti, an auspicious day for Hindus and traditionally observed as marking the onset of spring. As a child, he was called Naren for short, though his mother called him Biley, a name for the god Shiva. When he was born, his mother had considered naming him Vireshwar, after Shiva, but Narendranath was what he was called till the world came to know him as Swami Vivekananda.

His grandfather Durgadas was a reputed lawyer, but as the story goes, he renounced the world when he was but 25 years old. His father had made him a partner in the family law firm, and Durgadas was well educated, and well versed in Persian and Sanskrit. Yet his spiritual inclinations made him give it all up. He left his family and went to Benares (now Varanasi), leaving behind his wife Shyamasundari and young son Vishwanath. In that house full of relatives and well-wishers, it was Shyamasundari who brought up her son with great courage and fortitude.

Some years later, it is said, his wife Shyamasundari and their son made the journey to Benaras too, with other women from the family. Benaras was a pilgrimage site and it was considered auspicious to visit it in one's lifetime.

There are various versions for what happened thereafter. It is said that the boat they were in capsized, and Shyamasundari grabbed hold of her son to keep him afloat, fighting the strong river current as she did so. Her grip on her son's shoulder left a lasting mark. Apparently, she also met her husband on the steps of a temple, but he—already a hermit—turned away, after having recognized her. Another story goes that a few years later, a hermit came by their house. Such sadhus were never turned away, but were always given food or even shelter, but this one's arrival was greeted with some consternation. It was presumed it was the grandfather Durgadas who had come back again. He was kept locked up for three days before he managed to escape. It is also said that he blessed young Naren during this time.

Vishwanath followed his father's footsteps and became a lawyer too. He was kind-hearted and spiritually inclined. He also absorbed himself in intellectual pursuits; there were always discussions on at their house, and Naren was always privy to these even as a child. Just as his father, Vishwanath learnt Persian (then along with English, the official language of British-ruled Bengal), Arabic and also English. He loved quoting from the *Diwan-i-Hafiz*, the work of a 14th-century Persian poet whose poems spoke of love and faith, and against hypocrisy. Vishwanath, generous to a fault, was a magnanimous host and often held musical soirées. Narendranath inherited his love of music from his father. Vishwanath would sometimes engage his son in discussions and advised Narendranath to always be equable, no matter how delightful or trying the circumstances in his life.

Narendranath was the fourth child of his parents. An older brother had died in infancy. He had two older sisters. Of the ten Dutta children, seven grew to adulthood. As a child he learnt about piety and devotion from his mother, Bhuvaneshwari Devi. She devoted herself to the care of her family and others too. She had prayed to Shiva before he was born, and in one version, she had even dreamed that the god Shiva would be born as her son. When Naren was particularly naughty, his mother would pour water on his head, chanting verses in honour of Shiva. She would then berate herself half-mockingly, telling herself that the god Shiva had sent her one of his demons instead.

His mother would always serve other family members their meal first, before sitting down to eat. When a sadhu or an unexpected guest came by, she would make him feel welcome and go without food herself. She knew the epics and the sacred texts by heart and Naren learnt of these from the stories she would tell her children. He admired her patience and ability to do so much. Once he said that his mother 'would do a hundred of things, which I could not even do for five minutes'.

She told him that he must always remain devoted to the truth, no matter what the cost. Thus Naren grew up terrified of telling lies and fabricating falsehoods. He also learnt to be generous like his father and would give away everything to mendicants who stopped by. Once, after he gave away a new silk dhoti that had been gifted to him, he was locked up every time a sadhu wandered by.

He seemed to have inherited his spiritual leanings from his parents and grandfather, and his family, realizing his intentions, wanted him to get married. But he always managed to put it off.

A crisis came when Vishwanath Dutta passed away in 1884, of a long-standing heart ailment. The splendid house was divided up after his death. Naren was only 21 and had only just completed college. His father had been careless and too generous with his money, and the debts had piled up. It was hard for the Duttas, especially when one branch of the family including an old aunt who had lived with them for several years, filed a case claiming possession of the entire house. It took years for the suit to be settled, but these were difficult times for both Naren and his mother, for he was the oldest son and expected to shoulder the family's responsibilities.

Narendranath ensured his mother and younger siblings were cared for and it was only then that he, following his spiritual teacher or guru Shri Ramakrishna whom he met while still a student in college, took the vows of a *sanyasi* or a sadhu who had renounced the world.

It was in the late 1880s that he became a wandering monk and devoted his life to serving people, but he always remained devoted to his family, making sure they were well-provided for. However, his compassion and love spread much beyond his immediate family and encompassed the entire universe, especially the poor and downtrodden. He once spoke about his mother and all that he had learnt from her to an audience at Cambridge city in Massachusetts, USA. They later wrote to her at Christmas-time, appreciating her and all that she had imparted to her son, who was spreading the message of universal tolerance and understanding in all his public addresses and lectures.

As a boy, Naren loved animals too, and had several pets. There were white mice, a monkey, a goat, a peacock, and several pigeons. He remembered watching the mice play in their pen, running over the wheels time and time again: it taught him about the world, its constant movement and how every individual had to simply do his or her duty. Later, when he spent time at the Ramakrishna *math* or monastery at Belur, he had more pets to care for. He gave them names and spent time with them whenever he could.

There was a dog called Bagha, a she-goat named Hansi, an antelope, a stork, several cows, sheep, ducks and geese, and also a kid goat called Matru he was particularly fond of. It had a collar of little bells, and with it Narendranath ran and played like a child. He pretended Matru was related to him in a previous life and Matru even stayed in the same room as Narendranath. When Matru died he was inconsolable. Before milking the goat Hansi, he would gently ask its permission. Bagha the dog went to bathe in the river Ganga with other devotees on auspicious occasions. When Bagha died, he was buried in the grounds of the monastery. Once it had rained heavily in Calcutta and there was every danger of a flood, and so Narendranath wrote to a friend in the USA about his concern— and that included his pets too.

One of his younger brothers, Bhupendranath Dutta, wrote a book on him, calling Vivekananda a patriot and prophet. Bhupendranath had been a member of revolutionary militant groups like the Jugantar, and of the Ghadar party that sought to overthrow the British. An erstwhile member of the international communist group, Commintern, he later joined the Indian National Congress and worked for labourers and trade unions. Another younger brother, Mahendranath Dutta, too wrote a book on him and was a disciple of Shri Ramakrishna as well.

Some of Vivekananda's childhood joys continued to give him happiness later in life. He loved to sing, and also cooked for his fellow monks, friends and disciples, striving to get everything in the right measure. Once in Pasadena in California, USA, soon after he had completed a lecture, his disciples saw him deep in thought. They quietly followed a few steps behind, when suddenly he stopped, and shouted that he had found a solution. It turned out that he had just realized that mulligatawny soup acquired its unique taste from the bay leaf added to it for flavour!

Vivekananda grew to become one of India's foremost religious philosophers and social reformers. He travelled widely in India and in the West, introducing the philosophy of the ancient Hindu texts, as explained in Vedanta (the philosophical traditions concerned with interpreting the three basic texts of Hindu philosophy: the Upanishads, the Brahma Sutras and the Bhagavad Gita). He found a guru in Shri Ramakrishna and founded the Ramakrishna Mission in 1897 to do social work. He engaged monks and dedicated disciples to serve the poor and the needy in India. His message to erase ignorance and to broaden understanding between religions and nations, is an enduring one, and his birthday on 12 January is celebrated as National Youth Day across India.

# What Swami Vivekananda Said

Don't be ruffled if now and then you get a brush from the world; it will be over in no time, and everything will be all right.

**What I thought to be good yesterday, I do not think to be good now. When I look back upon my life and see what were my ideals at different times, I find this to be so. At one time my ideal was to drive a strong pair of horses; at another time I thought, if I could make a certain kind of sweetmeat, I should be perfectly happy; later I imagined that I should be entirely satisfied if I had a wife and children and plenty of money. Today, I laugh at all these ideals as mere childish nonsense.**

Hope is dominant in the heart of childhood. The whole world is a golden vision to the opening eyes of the child.

**Let positive, strong, helpful thoughts enter into your brains from very childhood. Lay yourselves open to these thoughts, and not to weakening and paralyzing ones.**

We only get what we deserve. It is a lie when we say, the world is bad and we are good.

**When I was a child I thought if I could be a cabman, it would be the very acme of happiness for me to drive about.**

Youth and beauty vanish, life and wealth vanish, name and fame vanish, even the mountains crumble into dust. Friendship and love vanish. Truth alone abides.

**From my childhood everyone around me taught weakness; I have been told ever since I was born that I was a weak thing. It is very difficult for me now to realize my own strength, but by analysis and reasoning I gain knowledge of my own strength; I realize it.**

We are what our thoughts have made us; so take care about what you think. Words are secondary. Thoughts live; they travel far.

**We are responsible for what we are, and whatever we wish ourselves to be, we have the power to make ourselves. If what we are now has been the result of our own past actions, it certainly follows that whatever we wish to be in the future can be produced by our present actions; so we have to know how to act.**

Learn everything that is good from others, but bring it in, and in your own way absorb it; do not become others.

**Education is the manifestation of perfection already existing in man.**

The whole life is a succession of dreams. My ambition is to be a conscious dreamer, that is all.

**The love which my mother gave to me has made me what I am, and I owe a debt to her that I can never repay.**

My huge stork is full of glee and so are the ducks and geese. My tame antelope fled from the *math* and gave us some days of anxiety in finding him. One of my ducks unfortunately died yesterday. She had been gasping for breath more than a week. One of my waggish old monks says, 'Sir, it is no use living in the Kaliyuga, when ducks catch cold from damp and rain, and frogs sneeze!'

# Gifts and Blessings

**N**arendranath gave every impression of being a prodigy, but his early childhood ambitions didn't stretch far. At one time, he wanted to be a coachman, for their turbans and fancy uniform impressed him no end. At other times, he expressed the desire to be a *halwai*, a sweetmeat maker, for then one could have delicious things to eat whenever one wanted.

One of the qualities that amazed everyone in his family and all his teachers first was his remarkable memory and ability to concentrate. He was able to remember anything he heard simply by hearing it once. He would never study much, but would recall everything, by dint of this gift.

As a child, it was also obvious that he was able to discipline his mind as if he was born with a yogic temperament. Sometimes he played at meditation, imagining he was a sage lost to the world and his family would find him rapt in prayer. On one occasion, he and a friend locked themselves in a room to meditate. It was a game Narendranath had devised, to see how long he could lose himself thinking of God, and in prayer. A long time passed and when there was no sign of them emerging or even a response when their names were called out, a search was launched for them. The door of the room they had locked themselves in had to be broken down, though his friend had fled the scene though the back door. Narendranath, however, still had his eyes closed, his body held rigidly straight in the traditional pose of the meditating sage.

Another day, he played in the same manner with his friends and as he sat lost in meditation with his eyes closed, oblivious to everything around him, a cobra came very close. While his friends screamed in fright and warning, Naren did not even blink, and remained engrossed in thought. The snake slithered away, while Narendranath remained unaware of it.

His first school was the local *pathshala* in the neighbourhood. Education was imparted in Bengali here. On his first day, he wore a dhoti, carried his own mat for all children had to sit on the mud floor, and there was a reed pen tied with a string to his waist. But his father was not very happy with the school, so Narendranath was also privately tutored at home. He learnt a little arithmetic, accounts, Sanskrit grammar, and Bengali. One day, the tutor found him at the table with his eyes closed, and he reprimanded Naren for dozing off. But Naren was able to recite the entire lesson for he had been listening intently as his teacher spoke. Once he memorized an entire book on ethics. Besides music and academics, Naren was also good at gymnastics.

When he was still a young boy, he accompanied his father and his family to Raipur in central India, where his father had taken on a new assignment as a lawyer. It was a long journey; at that time the railways did not cover most of India. They had to travel from Calcutta to Jabalpur in the Central Provinces and then on to to Raipur by bullock cart. In these two years, he was once again schooled at home but had little difficultly catching up on his studies when they returned once more to Calcutta. Here he was admitted into the Metropolitan Institute, set up by Ishwar Chandra Vidyasagar, the noted reformer and educationist. The school was open to everyone, even to those of lower castes, a revolutionary step at that time. Vidyasagar believed in women's education and widow remarriage, issues that made him initially unpopular and later widely revered.

Naren joined the Metropolitan Institute when he was seven. He had to dress more formally, but his trousers were always torn because of his restless ways and the games he was fond of such as playing with marbles, running and boxing, a sport at which he won several laurels. In the beginning, when told that he would have to learn English in this new school, he was upset, for to him English was still an unfamiliar language. But he was later convinced by an older relative who told him it would help him in later life. He, indeed, mastered the language and became an eloquent speaker, who would later impress audiences in the USA and in Europe with his perfect oration and fluency. The man who convinced him was the father of Ramachandra Datta, who would later introduce him to Shri Ramakrishna, the priest of the temple to the goddess Kali at Dakshineswar in Calcutta, and who was known for his deeply spiritual and humble ways. Shri Ramakrishna would later become Narendranath's spiritual teacher and guide.

At school, once Narendranath once got into a fight with a schoolmate, when the stronger boy snatched his *mithai* away. As he grew up, Vivekananda longed to take revenge, and dreamt of the time when he would be stronger and this would be possible. But when they were older, they became quite good friends instead. His mother's advice to him was to always believe in himself, especially if he knew that he was in the right.

As he loved music and had a good voice, Naren would organize plays and musicals. He was popular as a singer, and it was this that made Surendranath Mitra, one of Shri Ramakrishna's disciples, invite him over, and that's where he first met Shri Ramakrishna. He also enjoyed philosophical discussions and criticisms, and this was a constant feature in his home as well. His teachers soon learnt to put up with his constant questioning. He liked Sanskrit and grammar but did not much like Maths.

In school, he also organized mock durbars or courtrooms where he played the king. He was always the arbiter when his friends quarrelled. Besides playing with his pets, especially his dear white mice, he would busy himself making things. In Calcutta, the gas light had just been introduced on most streets, and Naren made his own toy gas works set, complete with pipes, earthen pots and bits of straw. He would experiment with cooking too, making dishes very spicy with a liberal use of red chilli powder. When he was in America, he enjoyed cooking for his disciples and students, substituting cayenne pepper for red chillies.

He took to cricket in school and won prizes for boxing. When he performed well at the entrance examination to college at the age of fifteen, the only student from Metropolitan who passed in the first division, his father gifted him a watch. He had topped his school despite having lost two years of studies when he was with his father in Raipur in central India.

In his last year at the Metropolitan Institute, the other students approached him to make a speech to honour a professor who was retiring. Professor Surendranath Banerjea, later a leading light of the Indian National Congress that would be formed in 1885 and the chairman of the Institute's board, was very impressed by Narendranath's address.

Narendranath enrolled first at Presidency College and then moved to the Scottish Church College, reading philosophy and history. He continued with his other interests too, setting up his own amateur theatre and performing in plays as Calcutta had a well organized theatre circuit. Once during a play, in which he was acting, it was apparent that the court's officer or the bailiff had come to arrest one of the leading actors. But Naren, thinking fast, spoke out in loud and ringing tones on the stage, pulling the official up for his daring and cheek. It amused everyone and embarrassed the officer thoroughly. Narendranath also charmed everyone by his singing. Later, in all his addresses and speeches, he would often sing, enchanting most of his listeners.

He was a skilled storyteller, and as a young man, he entertained everyone with his rendition of the old story from the 'Arabian Nights', *Ali Baba and the Forty Thieves*. He used his wide learning to good effect later, peppering his addresses and speeches with stories from the myths and sacred texts. He would also willingly help out his fellow students when they were in need. In college, one of the students was too poor to pay his fees. It was Narendranath who intervened with the college officials and requested that they allow him to take the examinations.

Before his graduation examinations in college, Narendranath spent a few days at his maternal grandfather's house in Calcutta. The exams were tough, but he knew all it would take was a few hours of rigorous concentration on his part. He would drink pots of tea and tie a string from a cot to his feet. If he fell asleep over his books and turned, the string would tighten and the movement would jerk him awake.

His many qualities and brilliance drew the notice of his teachers and fellow students. The principal of his college, Professor William Hastie, once spoke of his genius, adding that in all his travels, he had never come across another lad with quite as many talents as Narendranath. Hastie had taught philosophy to students in Germany, but Naren, he said, had more potential than any of them.

Narendranath completed his graduation in 1884, but it was the same year his father passed away after a heart ailment, leaving Narendranath and his family in deep shock and financial distress. His law studies, which he had enrolled in to become a lawyer like his father and grandfather, thus remained incomplete as it was now imperative that he being the eldest, find a job to support his family. He was only 21 and with his family, Narendranath endured great hardships and poverty during these years. It was during this time too that he met Shri Ramakrishna, a mystic and spiritual seeker who was the priest of the temple at Dakshineswar, and his search for spiritual meaning took on greater urgency when he asked Shri Ramakrishna several questions about the existence of God. It made Narendranath curious and eager to study the ancient Hindu philosophical texts to find his own answers to such things. Besides Shri Ramakrishna, whom he accepted and revered as his teacher and mentor, Narendranath was always keen to learn from renowned teachers and scholars, especially those who had a mastery of the old Sanskrit texts and philosophies. His ability to concentrate and his remarkable memory meant he impressed all those he learnt from.

During his travels through India after Shri Ramakrishna's death in 1886, he stopped at Jaipur in Rajputana, as the princely states then comprising present-day Rajasthan were called. Here he approached a scholar to learn the intricacies of Sanskrit grammar, but the man, for all his knowledge, was not a good teacher. When the scholar was unable to explain something to Narendranath, the former was annoyed with himself. Narendranath then decided to teach himself. An aphorism in the text had to be explained, but the commentary on it was much too detailed. Yet he put aside all thoughts of food and sleep and proceeded to master the commentary, much to his teacher's surprise the next day.

His remarkable ability to concentrate was apparent in several different events in his life, when he could simply immerse himself in a situation and emerge triumphant. The Raja of Khetri, a princely states in Rajputana was one of Narendranath's staunchest admirers and disciples. According to one of Narendranath's disciples, who was close to him, it was the Raja of Khetri who had suggested, before Narendranath's departure to the USA, the name Vivekananda— *vivek* means wisdom and *ananda* means bliss or joy—and this was the name by which Narendranath soon came to be called and recognized the world over.

On his visit to Chicago, USA, in 1893 when the Parliament of World Religions was held, he once took a stroll along a river. That day as he walked along the river, he saw a few boys with airguns aiming at eggshells strewn on the waters. They were rather ineffectual in their attempts. As the shells only rolled up and down, and turned over on the choppy waters, not one of the boys struck the mark, despite several attempts. When they saw him watching their game with great interest, the boys invited him to try. He took the gun one of the boys held out and then concentrated on the bobbing and floating eggshells for a long time. When he fired, he struck an eggshell every time. The boys, surprised and very impressed, wanted to know if he was a skilled shooter and had had lots of practice. But Vivekananda let them into his secret, advising them to concentrate on whatever they were doing, and not think of anything else. It was a lesson, he told them, which would be of use to them in whatever else they did too.

In another small American town that he had visited to deliver a lecture, he had another strange experience. Here, he was accosted by a several college students who wanted to challenge him. They lived on a nearby ranch and had heard him speak of concentration and all the powers it bestowed. Vivekananda had even said that if a man concentrated enough, he could be totally oblivious of the outside world. The boys wanted to test him and invited Vivekananda to speak to them. In the hall, they placed a wooden tub, turned up to serve as a platform for Vivekananda. Soon he began speaking and was lost in his subject. He totally missed the fact that stray empty shots were being fired in his direction, and while the bullets went streaming past his ears, he heard nothing. Instead he continued speaking without pause. When it was all over, the young men stood around him in amazement, and praised his abilities.

Later, he wrote about the quality of concentration in his book on Jnana Yoga. Vivekananda wrote in detail about the quality of mindfulness, which is the ability to pay full attention to what really mattered, and which was a step towards gaining knowledge.

All his life he remained a keen student and was always eager to teach himself new things. On a visit to Switzerland in 1896, he wrote to an associate in Calcutta about a book written in Tamil and published in Mysore. It contained all the 108 Upanishads. Vivekananda had seen it in the library of the noted scholar, Professor Paul Deussen, and wanted a copy. He asked for a copy in the Devanagari script, in which Hindi, Bengali and other north Indian languages were written. However, if one was not available, he wrote that the Tamil one would do just as well. He would simply teach himself the language. He asked his associate to write the Tamil letters and compounds, and juxtapose these with their Devanagari equivalents, so that he could teach himself the Tamil language too!

# What Swami Vivekananda Said

Take up one idea. Make that one idea your life—think of it, dream of it, live on that idea. Let the brain, muscles, nerves, every part of your body, be full of that idea, and just leave every other idea alone. This is the way to success.

**Do not believe in a thing because you have read about it in a book. Do not believe in a thing because another man has said it was true. Do not believe in words because they are hallowed by tradition. Find out the truth for yourself. Reason it out. That is realization.**

Even the greatest fool can accomplish a task if it were after his or her heart. But the intelligent ones are those who can convert every work into one that suits their taste.

**From contentment comes superlative happiness.**

Great occasions rouse even the lowest of human beings to some kind of greatness, but he alone is the really great man whose character is great always, the same wherever he be.

**This is the first lesson to learn: be determined not**

**to curse anything outside, not to lay the blame upon anyone outside, but stand up, lay the blame on yourself. You will find that is always true. Get hold of yourself.**

This life is a hard fact; work your way through it boldly, though it may be adamantine; no matter, the soul is stronger.

**The constitutional belief in freedom is the basis of all reasoning.**

Those who grumble at the little thing that has fallen to their lot to do will grumble at everything. Always grumbling, they will lead a miserable life, and everything will be a failure. But those who do their duties as they go, putting their shoulders to the wheel, will see the light, and higher duties will fall to their share.

**Those who work at a thing heart and soul not only achieve success in it but through their absorption in that they also realize the supreme truth—Brahman. Those who work at a thing with their whole heart receive help from God.**

The mind has to be made malleable like clay. Just as clay sticks wherever you throw it, so the mind must be made to dwell upon whatever object you concentrate it.

**Concentration is the essence of all knowledge, nothing can be done without it.**

The will is not free—it is a phenomenon bound by cause and effect—but there is something behind the will which is free.

**A man of science rises, he is thirsting after knowledge. No sacrifice is too great, no struggle too hopeless for him.**

The more this power of concentration, the more knowledge is acquired, because this is the one and only method of acquiring knowledge.

**The powers of the mind are like the rays of the sun: when they are concentrated, they illumine.**

Books are infinite in number and time is short. The secret of knowledge is to take what is essential. Take that and try to live up to it.

**Believe nothing until you find it out for yourself; that is what it teaches us. Truth requires no prop to make it stand.**

It is wrong to believe blindly. You must exercise your own reason and judgment; you must practise, and see whether these things happen or not.

**The world is ready to give up its secrets if we only know how to knock, how to give it the necessary blow. The strength and force of the blow come through concentration.**

Do one thing at a time, and while doing it put your whole soul into it to the exclusion of all else.

**All knowledge that the world has ever received comes from the mind; the infinite library of the universe is in our own mind.**

There is no limit to the power of the human mind. The more concentrated it is, the more power is brought to bear on one point.

**If you want to study your own mind, it will be the same process. You will have to concentrate your mind and turn it back upon itself. The difference in this world between mind and mind is simply the fact of concentration. One, more concentrated than the other, gets more knowledge.**

In the lives of all great men, past and present, we find this tremendous power of concentration. Those are men of genius, you say. The science of Yoga tells us that we are all geniuses if we try hard to be . . . The same power is in everyone.

Concentration, of course, comes from various sources. Through the senses you can get concentration. Some get it when they hear beautiful music, others when they see beautiful scenery . . . . Some get concentrated by lying upon beds of spikes, sharp iron spikes, others by sitting upon sharp pebbles.

Great undertakings are always fraught with many obstacles. It is these obstacles which knock and shape great characters . . .

The man who says that he will work when the world has become all good and then he will enjoy bliss is as likely to succeed as the man who sits beside the Ganga and says, 'I will ford the river when all the water has run into the ocean.'

Who makes us ignorant? We ourselves. We put our hands over our eyes and weep that it is dark.

Why are people so afraid? The answer is that they have made themselves helpless and dependent on others. We are so lazy, we do not want to do anything ourselves. We want a Personal God, a Saviour or a Prophet to do everything for us.

The ideal of all education, all training, should be this man-making. But, instead of that, we are always trying to polish up the outside. What use in polishing up the outside when there is no inside? The end and aim of all training is to make the man grow.

**One of the greatest lessons I have learnt in my life is to pay as much attention to the means of work as to its end . . .**

Our great defect in life is that we are so much drawn to the ideal, the goal is so much more enchanting, so much more alluring, so much bigger on our mental horizon, that we lose sight of the details altogether.

**But whenever failure comes, if we analyse it critically, in ninety-nine per cent of cases we shall find that it was because we did not pay attention to the means. Proper attention to the finishing, strengthening, of the means is what we need. With the means all right, the end must come.**

The means are the cause: attention to the means, therefore, is the great secret of life. We also read this in the Gita and learn that we have to work, constantly work with all our power; to put our whole mind in the work, whatever it be, that we are doing. At the same time, we must not be attached.

To succeed, you must have tremendous perseverance, tremendous will. 'I will drink the ocean,' says the persevering soul, 'at my will mountains will crumble up.' Have that sort of energy, that sort of will; work hard, and you will reach the goal.

The man who gives way to anger, or hatred, or any other passion, cannot work; he only breaks himself to pieces, and does nothing practical. It is the calm, forgiving, equable, well-balanced mind that does the greatest amount of work.

Be free; hope for nothing from anyone. I am sure if you look back upon your lives you will find that you were always vainly trying to get help from others, which never came. All the help that has come was from within yourselves. You only had the fruits of what you yourselves worked for, and yet you were strangely hoping all the time for help.

Arise! Awake! And stop not until the goal is reached.

# A Compassionate Heart

As a child, Narendranath saw his mother donate generously to anyone who came to their doorstep. He once saw his mother come to the help of a Muslim family who were their tenants. She agreed to waive their rent when the family's breadwinner died. She also tore up the title deed so they could live there, reassured. Being witness to his parents' acts of kindness and his own experience with poverty made him sensitive to the poor and their sufferings. He learnt early on from his mother that one could find fulfilment in helping and serving others.

His father, a lawyer, had many clients. Often they and other visitors would assemble in the *baithak* or living room, reclining on cushions. Naren noticed that everyone had a different hookah or smoking pipe, and no one could use another's. It puzzled him and one day he took a whiff from everyone's hookah, for he wondered if any would taste different. His actions caused some consternation, though Naren realized that the whiff seemed the same in each case. He learnt only later that owing to differences of caste and religion, everyone had to have their own hookahs. On another occasion, he shocked everyone when he accepted *sandesh*, a sweet, offered by a Muslim client of his father's.

This same client would often regale him with fairy stories involving caravans and hunts on elephants. He made Naren believe that he had undertaken such travels himself and promised to take Naren along once he was taller. But he would put off Naren each time on the pretext that he was still short by an inch to meet the expedition's requirements!

It was acquaintances such as these that made Naren realize the essential humanity that lay in every individual. He found that differences of caste and religion were superficial, and created to divide people. Even in his learning of music, he bridged differences, learning from masters of two different styles, Ahmad Khan and Beni Gupta.

His compassion made him reach out to help those he saw in need. As a young teenager, he had once gone for an outing by the river Ganga with some of his friends. As things happened, one of them soon fell too sick to take the carriage back home. Naren stayed behind with him, and let the rest carry on. Another time, he went to a fair and bought Shiva idols for himself. On his way home, he saw a small boy come in the way of a horse carriage. Tossing his cherished idols with no further thought, he pulled away the boy just in time, as the carriage galloped past. On another occasion, a friend in college was too poor to pay his fees and the administrators warned him that his name would be struck off the college rolls. Naren interceded before a college official on his friend's behalf, asking him to reconsider the decision, and it all ended well for his friend.

As a boy, he had never been short of anything, but his father's death introduced him to poverty. Narendranath was only 21 years old then. His father had been a generous and kind-hearted person and supported many relatives, some of them good for nothing. But his father had left behind too many debts and all at once the family was plunged into despair as it became difficult to make ends meet. Those were hard times and Narendranath tried to alleviate his family's difficulties as best as he could, and silently bore his own hardships.

Sometimes he would be away at a friend's house and refuse the meal offered him, as he could not eat when his mother and siblings were hungry. At home he would refuse food, pretending that he had already eaten, so his family could eat his share instead. He looked desperately for a job and had doors slammed in his face, but he never gave up. For some months he worked in a lawyer's office and also taught in the school set up by Ishwar Chandra Vidyasagar. Though he felt his family's suffering and strived hard to help them, he refused the suggestions of some of his friends who had at time resorted to unfair means, to earn something.

During these years he sought spiritual solace in attending Shri Ramakrishna's sermons or in meeting him, as he did often. But he consented to become Shri Ramakrishna's disciple only after the latter had assured him that his family would not want for anything. He remained concerned about his family even when he had taken a monk's vows, and renounced the world to become a *sanyasi*. He would write to his mother often and spoke of her frequently in the addresses and speeches he made later.

When his teacher Shri Ramakrishna passed away in 1886, he left his young disciples in Narendranath's care. They lived in an abandoned house in Baranagore in Calcutta that had been bought for them by one of Shri Ramakrishna's disciples. They lived very austere and simple lives, and often forgot their food when absorbed in meditation, worship, study, or devotional music. Often there would be no food at all, or only rice, with not even salt nor bitter herbs for flavouring; and on such occasions they spent days in prayer and meditation. It was at these times that Narendranath kept their spirits up, teaching them and also taking care of them.

He introduced them to different systems of philosophies and ethics. He spoke of the ancient Greek philosophers, especially Plato and Aristotle. The former's contribution to how knowledge comes into being or how we acquire knowledge and Aristotle's unique contribution in formulating logic as a subject is enduring in several ways. Their thought was picked up later philosophers who lived in the 18th century, such as Immanuel Kant and Georg Friedrich Hegel. Kant believed in the predominance of one's reasoning in perceiving everything, and Hegel followed this up, though he also emphasized the role of morals and one's duty in decision-making. Vivekananda explained to his disciples what the Buddha's philosophy was all about, and also the doctrine of Advaita, built around the interpretation of the Vedas and the Upanishads, as developed by the Hindu philosophers such as Adi Shankara, Madhavacharya and Ramanuja. Shankara wrote about the Supreme Soul (*Brahman*) in which all individual souls were ultimately subsumed, Madhavacharya stressed the importance of knowledge in seeking the Divine, and Ramanuja laid the foundations of Bhakti philosophy with its emphasis on devotion. These rigorous discussions were relieved by hours of music, in which Vivekananda led them all.

In his days as a wandering monk, as he travelled across India, he found himself—especially when it was dark or he was exhausted—compelled to seek shelter in the houses of the poor and those who belonged to the lower castes. The latter were often forced to live outside the villages, and fend for themselves, but Vivekananda had no hesitation in accepting their hospitality and considered himself blessed for it. He would describe this in his letters to his disciples and associates, narrating how they made him welcome though they barely had enough to live on. It was the generosity shown by the poor towards him, in spite of all the ostracism they faced, that made Vivekananda determined to work for the reform and regeneration of Indian society. Many years later when he earned some money on his lecture tours in America, he would at times donate his money to the poor and the needy.

His travels once took him to Mount Abu in Rajputana where he accepted the hospitality of a Muslim official, an act that shocked many. But Vivekananda stuck fast to what he had learnt, that everyone was essentially the same. In Khetri, the king once arranged a performance by a dancing girl. Vivekananda however refused to be part of such festivities, for as a monk he had renounced such worldly pleasures. But the dancer's song reached him through the walls, a sad, plaintive song about the world seeing her as evil but that it was her life and her duty to perform for the pleasure of her audience. The song and its words moved him to tears. He realized there was divinity in everyone, and he must never discriminate.

Before he left for America for the first time in 1893, Narendranath's mother prepared a special dinner for him.

When it was over, she offered him a dish of fruits and a knife. As Narendranath cut the fruit with his knife, his mother asked for the knife. When he handed it over, she told him that he had passed the test and explained that he had given it to her keeping the sharp edge turned towards himself. The gesture, though small and almost insignificant, told her that he was careful and considerate of others, and would always be so in important matters of life too.

He travelled to the USA, hoping to be part of the Parliament of World Religions that was being organized in Chicago. He wanted to tell the world about Hindu philosophy and arouse awareness about India's past greatness and her present plight. His initial days in the USA, however, were hard and he was often short of money. Fortunately, he found friends and others willing to help and in a few weeks, he found himself comfortable. But he was always aware of the poverty of many of his fellow Indians lived in, and this drove him to tears on many an occasion. He was offered a teaching position at the universities at Columbia and Harvard, but he knew he had to return and devote himself to the service of the people in his country. His heart would always be with the poor and neglected people of India.

During the latter part of 1901, as a new monastery was being built for the monks of the Ramakrishna Mission, he came across a number of workers who were of Santhali origin, an ethnic group from central India. They were occupied in levelling the grounds around the new monastery at Belur in Calcutta. Vivekananda would often stop and talk to them and found great joy in listening to their stories and accounts of their life. One day he arranged a feast for them and served them himself. The meal had delicacies they had never tasted before and Vivekananda felt a special joy in seeing their happiness. He said later that he had served God Himself by feeding the workers.

His compassion meant that he reached out to strangers, helping them readily and unhesitatingly. In his days in Chicago, where he stayed behind for a few weeks after the Parliament of Religions, he would go for a walk in the park. Sometimes he would sit on a bench, and it was on one such occasion, a young American woman with her daughter came by. She said she had some errands to run, and he watched over her daughter till she had completed them. This happened a few other times and he soon became friends with the woman and her daughter.

Sometime after his return from the west, he explained to a disciple who was somewhat sceptical about the possibility of there ever being harmony among India's diverse groups. Vivekananda only replied that years of travel and austerities had taught him that God or divinity was present in all beings. And serving all beings was to him an act of worship. He was willing to live in poverty, just so he could serve others. When a fellow disciple asked him where he would get funds, Vivekananda replied that if the need arose, the land belonging to the Belur monastery would be sold to serve the poor.

He was feted universally in return. He received a rousing reception wherever he went—at Kandy, Anuradhapuram, Jaffna, Pamban, Rameswaram, Ramnad, Paramakkudi, Madurai, Trichinopoly, and

Kumbakonam, Madras and finally Calcutta—it showed how deeply he had endeared himself to everyone.

He received a touching welcome from his disciple, the Raja of Ramnad, near Rameswaram in south India. Here at Ramnad, the horses were unhitched from the carriage that carried him, and everyone including the king held the reins and drew his carriage. At Rameswaram the king erected, in the Swami's honour, a four-foot high victory column with a suitable inscription. At a small railroad station near Madras, hundreds of people gathered for a glimpse of Vivekananda. The stationmaster did not want to delay the train since no stop was scheduled. But the crowd of admirers flung themselves on the track, and the train had to be halted to allow the people to greet Vivekananda.

He would serve his disciples too on occasion. One Wednesday, which was the day of Ekadashi or the eleventh day of the moon and a day marked by fasting and observance of religious rites, he fasted too. He insisted, however, on serving Sister Nivedita, who was his disciple, her morning meal. It was a simple meal of boiled jackfruit seeds, boiled potatoes, plain rice, and cold milk and then at the meal's end, he himself poured the water over Sister Nivedita's hands, and dried them with a towel. He mentioned the Biblical story when Jesus had washed his disciples' feet.

As things unfortunately turned out, Swami Vivekananda passed away a few days after this event. His disciples believed he had attained *samadhi* in his search for the Divine. In his young life, he travelled widely, wrote a lot, and worked incessantly not merely in search of spiritualism but to serve the cause of mankind.

# What Swami Vivekananda Said

All love is expansion, all selfishness is contraction. Love is therefore the only law of life. He who loves lives, he who is selfish is dying. Therefore, love for love's sake, because it is the only law of life, just as you breathe to live.

**Strength is Life, Weakness is Death**
**Expansion is Life, Contraction is Death.**
**Love is Life, Hatred is Death.**

Bless people when they revile you. Think how much good they are doing by helping to stamp out the false ego.

**This world will always continue to be a mixture of good and evil. Our duty is to sympathize with the weak and to love even the wrongdoer.**

The more we grow in love, virtue and holiness, the more we see love, virtue and holiness outside.

**There is no virtue higher than non-injury.**

Everyone can play the role of a master, but it is very difficult to be a servant.

An American thinks that whatever an American does in accordance with the custom of his country is the best thing to do, and that whoever does not follow his custom must be a very wicked man. A Hindu thinks that his customs are the only right ones and are the best in the world, and that whosoever does not obey them must be the most wicked man living. This is quite a natural mistake which all of us are apt to make. But it is very harmful; it is the cause of half the uncharitableness found in the world . . . Much of the oppression of powerful nations on weaker ones is caused by this prejudice. It dries up their fellow-feeling for fellow men.

We should always try to see the duty of others through their own eyes, and never judge the customs of other peoples by our own standard. I am not the standard of the universe. I have to accommodate myself to the world, and not the world to me.

We must have friendship for all; we must be merciful toward those that are in misery; when people are happy, we ought to be happy; and to the wicked we must be indifferent. These attitudes will make the mind peaceful.

The same thing which is producing misery in one, may

produce happiness in another. The fire that burns the child, may cook a good meal for a starving man.

**Why do we see wickedness? There was a stump of a tree, and in the dark, a thief came that way and said, 'That is a policeman.' A young man waiting for his beloved saw it and thought that it was his sweetheart. A child who had been told ghost stories took it for a ghost and began to shriek. But all the time it was the stump of a tree. We see the world as we are.**

Now know once and for all that I do not care for name or fame, or any humbug of that type. I want to preach my ideas for the good of the world.

**Give up all desire and be at peace. Have neither friends nor foes, and live alone. Thus shall we travel having neither friends nor foes, neither pleasure nor pain, neither desire nor jealousy, injuring no creatures, being the cause of injury to no creatures—from mountain to mountain, from village to village, preaching the name of the Lord.**

In criticizing another, we always foolishly take one especially brilliant point as the whole of our life and compare that with the dark ones in the life of another. Thus we make mistakes in judging individuals.

**I am persuaded that a leader is not made in one life. He has to be born for it. For the difficulty is not in organisation and making plans; the test, the real test of the leader lies in holding widely different people together along the line of their common sympathies. And this can only be done unconsciously, never by trying.**

Mercy is heaven itself; to be good, we have all to be merciful. Even justice and right should stand on mercy.

**Mercy shall not be for men alone, but shall go beyond, and embrace the whole world.**

The true philosopher strives to destroy nothing, but to help all.

**Seek no help from high or low, from above or below. Desire nothing—and look upon this vanishing panorama as a witness and let it pass.**

This world will always be a mixture of good and evil, of happiness and misery; this wheel will ever go up and come down; dissolution and resolution is the inevitable law. Blessed are those who struggle to go beyond.

**The world is full of the talk of love, but it is hard to love. Where is love? How do you know that there is love? The first test of love is that it knows no**

bargaining. So long as you see a man love another only to get something from him, you know that that is not love; it is shopkeeping. Wherever there is any question of buying and selling, it is not love.

Love cannot come through fear; its basis is freedom. When we really begin to love the world, then we understand what is meant by brotherhood or mankind, and not before.

. . . In this world everything depends upon one's words. To get an insight behind the words . . . is not given to all, and one must associate long with a man to be able to understand him . . . .

Our watchword, then, will be acceptance, and not exclusion. Not only toleration, for so-called toleration is often blasphemy, and I do not believe in it. I believe in acceptance. Why should I tolerate? Toleration means that I think that you are wrong and I am just allowing you to live.

Everyone must be judged according to his own ideal, and not by that of anyone else. In our dealings with our fellow-beings we constantly labour under this mistake, and I am of the opinion that the vast majority of our quarrels with one another arise simply from this one cause that we are always trying to judge others' gods by our own, others' ideals by our ideals, and others' motives by our motives.

# A Courageous Life

n his book, *Discovery of India*, Jawaharlal Nehru, independent India's first prime minister, wrote about Vivekananda. He mentioned that the one quality that truly described Vivekananda was that he was fearless in everything. Vivekananda believed that it was courage that made one undertake the impossible and succeed in such endeavours as well.

Courage wasn't something Vivekananda acquired. Even as a boy, he showed it in ample measure. There was a tree in a friend's garden that Naren, as an eight-year-old, was particularly fond of climbing. This was a *champaka* tree, known for its fragrant yellow and white flowers. Naren would climb onto its branches and dangle head down in the manner of the vampires or *betaals* he had read about. His friend's grandfather was worried that the boys would hurt themselves and also very irritated, for the flowers were especially used on auspicious occasions and offered to the gods. A vigorous shaking of the branches would dislodge the flowers and send them plummeting downward.

To dissuade the boys, he told them that a ghost lived in the branches and he was known to wring the necks of boys who dared disturb him. At night, the elderly man went on, to the consternation of his wide-eyed young listeners, the ghost appeared in white and presented a fearsome spectacle. The story frightened the other boys, but Narendranath did not lose his composure. He only asked the older man if he had indeed seen the ghost, but the latter walked away, repeating his dire warnings. The very next day, Naren climbed the tree while his friends stood below, crying out their warnings. They warned him to watch out for the wrathful ghost who was now sure to twist his neck for all his daring. But Naren only laughed as he climbed higher onto its branches. He said his friends were being fools for if the older man's story was true, the ghost would have done so long ago.

It was courage that made him keep his head when his friends would lose hope. For instance, when he was still in school, a British warship stopped in Calcutta harbour and people were allowed in, with a permit. Naren and his friends queued up in excitement but a lower official at the door said young people would not be allowed on the ship. While his friends turned away disappointed, Naren did not give up. He spotted a door, behind which another flight of steps led up and he followed his instincts and walked up to the first floor, where he soon found himself in the chambers of the senior official. He placed the permit paper before him, as the official attended simultaneously to other things, and got his signature allowing them entry.

Narendranath stood up for his principles and convictions, even before his teachers. Even in his early boyhood, he demanded to be convinced. Once Vidyasagar, the founder of the Metropolitan Institute where Narendranath was a student, reprimanded his teacher when Naren was unjustly punished for asking too many questions. On another occasion he was caned by a teacher who thought he was being impudent and cheeky. Though he was upset, his mother consoled him. She advised him that no matter the consequences, he had to stand up for what he believed was right. It was advice Naren followed all his life and he was always unafraid of speaking his mind before anyone.

As he wandered around the country as a monk, he stopped once at Sarnath, in central India. It was a place holy to Buddhism for this was where, more than 1,500 years ago, the Buddha had preached his first sermon after attaining nirvana. There was a temple there dedicated to the Goddess Durga and it was when he came out from it that Narendranath was accosted by a troop of ferocious monkeys. They followed him, screeched shrilly and threatened to claw him any moment, when a sadhu shouted across to him that he must turn back and look the monkeys squarely in the eye. 'Face them,' was the advice of the old sage. Narendranath stopped running and realized what the other man was trying to say. He stood tall and glared back at the irate monkeys, who at once dropped their gaze and their aggression, and melted away into the trees. It was a lesson he would always remember.

When he stopped at Alwar in Rajputana, he had a sharp exchange of words with the Maharaja, who wanted progress in his kingdom but was known to blindly adopt western methods, even when these went against time-honoured traditions of his kingdom and people. The king asked Narendranath why he roamed the country almost like a vagabond when he was able-bodied and educated enough to make a living otherwise. To this, Vivekananda asked the king why the latter preferred the company of Englishmen and went on hunting excursions with them when he had other royal duties to attend to. The surprised king replied that it was because he liked doing so, though he could find no other reason and Vivekananda smiled, for the king had his answer.

The king also mocked the practice of image worship and idolatry for, in his view, these were but mere figures of stone, clay or metal and had no godlike powers. Vivekananda's explanation that the images were symbols for the gods people held sacred, fell on deaf ears. Then Vivekananda asked the king's prime minister for the king's portrait and when this was produced, he asked the prime minister to spit on it. The poor man, after much hesitation, did so, as the audience looked on in horror, fearing the most terrible punishment for Vivekananda as well as the king's prime minister. But the gesture was not missed. The king realized that while it was but a picture it represented him in every way and people thus accorded it respect. In a similar way, the image of the deity helped the worshipper concentrate on his worship and prayer. The king realized his mistake and apologized to Narendranath.

Narendranath would also never leave friends in times of distress or when they were in danger. He travelled to England in 1895, and one day was walking across some fields with a disciple, Miss Henrietta Müller, and an English friend when a raging bull came tearing towards them. The Englishman simply turned and ran with no further thought. He soon reached the other side of the field safely and climbed over the fence in relief. Miss Müller too ran as far as she could and then her legs gave way in fatigue. She sank to the ground, as the bull charged on towards her. Vivekananda saw all this and realized he too couldn't put up much resistance against an enraged bull. But he bent down, picked up two small stones and rubbed them against each other, saying he felt strong and unshaken for he had firm faith in god and himself—and stood there. Later Vivekananda described how he had busied himself thinking over a mathematical calculation, wondering how far the bull would be able to throw him. But the animal did something surprising, it suddenly stopped when barely a few paces away, and then lifting its head, strode sullenly off in a different direction. The Englishman returned, abashed at his cowardice while a grateful Miss Müller could only wonder at Vivekananda's ability to muster up courage in a difficult situation.

It was this spirit that never deserted him even when he faced poverty and difficult circumstances. When he travelled to the USA, he faced immense difficulties in the beginning. The money he had soon dwindled for things were more expensive there. There was a time when he even slept in a freight car outside the Chicago railway station as he forgotten the address of the venue where the Parliament was scheduled to be held. The next few days were terrible, as his money was running out, he had lost the directions to the venue and he was also very hungry and exhausted. He tried to ask for help, and for food, in the time-honoured tradition of monks but had the door shut in his face.

However, he did not lose hope. As he rested on a sidewalk, a woman from the house opposite noticed him and from his robes conjectured he was a participant at the Parliament. It was this lady, Mrs George Hale, who took him to the conference herself and the

Hale family were soon to become lifelong friends and associates of Vivekananda. He kept up a long correspondence with them, especially the two Hale daughters, Mary and Harriet, and their cousins, Isabelle and Harriet McKindley.

Soon after his addresses at the Parliament of World Religions in Chicago, he gave several other lectures, where he was eloquent, passionate and outspoken. While he was praised highly in many quarters and soon had many admirers and committed followers, some of his forthright words riled the conservative sections of his audience. They were not many but they were very vocal in their criticism of Vivekananda. These included some missionaries and their American patrons. Angered by his words that criticized fanatics of all religions, they opted to vilify and mock him in newspapers and magazines and also in private. There were times when false stories casting aspersions on his character were also planted in newspapers. When his alarmed friends and disciples in India sent him these clippings and wrote to him letters of advice, he laughed it off. He also said that most Americans were not like that and that he had been received with cordiality and warmth wherever he had gone. He was able to set up the Ramakrishna Mission in 1897 to work for the cause of India's welfare, and also to promote understanding between the East and the West, also because of the able support and assistance from his friends in the West.

# What Swami Vivekananda Said

The greatest religion is to be true to your own nature. Have faith in yourselves.

**Dare to be free, dare to go as far as your thought leads, and dare to carry that out in your life.**

Never think there is anything impossible for the soul. It is the greatest heresy to think so. If there is sin, this is the only sin; to say that you are weak, or others are weak.

**The Vedanta recognizes no sin; it only recognizes error. And the greatest error, says the Vedanta, is to say that you are weak, that you are a sinner, a miserable creature, and that you have no power and you cannot do this and that.**

Be not afraid, for all great power throughout the history of humanity has been with the people. From out of their ranks have come all the greatest geniuses of the world, and history can only repeat itself. Be not afraid of anything. You will do marvellous work.

**Comfort is no test of truth. Truth is often far from being comfortable.**

We know how often in our lives through laziness and cowardice we give up the battle and try to hypnotize our minds into the belief that we are brave.

**All weakness, all bondage, is imagination.**

The fire that warms us can also consume us; it is not the fault of the fire.

**We reap what we sow. We are the makers of our own fate. The wind is blowing; those vessels whose sails are unfurled catch it, and go forward on their way, but those which have their sails furled do not catch the wind. Is that the fault of the wind? . . . We make our own destiny.**

Each work has to pass through these stages—ridicule, opposition, and then acceptance. Those who think ahead of their time are sure to be misunderstood.

**Whatever you think, that you will be. If you think yourself weak, weak you will be; if you think yourself strong, you will be. Anything that makes you weak—physically, intellectually and spiritually— reject it as poison.**

The whole secret of existence is to have no fear. Never fear what will become of you, depend on no one. Only the moment you reject all help are you freed.

We must learn that nothing can happen to us, unless we make ourselves susceptible to it.

When once you consider an action, do not let anything dissuade you. Consult your heart, not others, and then follow its dictates.

Strength, power, and courage are things which are very peculiar. We generally say, 'A courageous man, a brave man, a daring man, but we must bear in mind that that courage or bravery or any other trait does not always characterise the man. The same man who would rush to the mouth of a cannon shrinks from the knife of the surgeon; and another man who never dares to face a gun will calmly bear a severe surgical operation, if need be. Now, in judging others you must always define your terms of courage or greatness. The man whom I am criticizing as not good may be wonderfully so in some points in which I am not.

The brave alone can afford to be sincere.

Whenever we attain a higher vision, the lower vision disappears of itself.

This I have seen in life—those who are overcautious about themselves fall into dangers at every step; those who are afraid of losing honour and respect, get only disgrace; and those who are always afraid of loss, always lose.

**There never has been a blow undeserved: there never has been an evil for which I did not pave the way with my own hands. We ought to know that. Analyse yourselves and you will find that every blow you have received, came to you because you prepared yourselves for it. You did half, and the external world did the other half: that is how the blow came.**

All power is within you; you can do anything and everything. Believe in that, do not believe that you are weak; do not believe that you are half-crazy lunatics, as most of us do nowadays. You can do anything and everything, without even the guidance of anyone. Stand up and express the divinity within you.

**Be not afraid of anything. You will do marvellous work. It is fearlessness that brings Heaven even in a moment.**

The greatest sin is to think yourself weak.

**Desire, ignorance, and inequality—this is the trinity of bondage.**

Believe in yourself and the world will be at your feet.

**The Vedanta recognizes no sin, it only recognizes error. And the greatest error, says the Vedanta, is to say that you are weak, that you are a sinner, a miserable creature, and that you have no power and you cannot do this and that.**

The cheerful mind perseveres and the strong mind hews its way through a thousand difficulties.

**Take risks in your life; If you win, you can lead! If you lose, you can guide!**

If faith in ourselves had been more extensively taught and practised, I am sure a very large portion of the evils and miseries that we have would have vanished.

**The only religion that ought to be taught is the religion of fearlessness. Either in this world or in the world of religion, it is true that fear is the sure cause of degradation and sin. It is fear that brings misery, fear that brings death, fear that breeds evil. And what causes fear? Ignorance of our own nature.**

In a day, when you don't come across any problems—

you can be sure that you are travelling on a wrong path.

**There is no help for you outside of yourself; you are the creator of the universe. Like the silkworm you have built a cocoon around yourself . . . . Burst your own cocoon and come out as the beautiful butterfly, as the free soul. Then alone you will see Truth.**

Don't look back—forward, infinite energy, infinite enthusiasm, infinite daring, and infinite patience—then alone can great deeds be accomplished.

**The brain and muscles must develop simultaneously. Iron nerves with an intelligent brain—and the whole world is at your feet.**

There are two sorts of courage. One is the courage of facing the cannon. And the other is the courage of spiritual conviction.

**Bear in mind . . . that only cowards and those who are weak commit sin and tell lies. The brave are always moral. Try to be moral, try to be brave, try to be sympathising.**

Stand up, be bold, be strong. Take the whole responsibility on your own shoulders, and know that you are the creator of your own destiny. All the strength and succour you want is within yourselves. Therefore make your own future.

**We are forever trying to make our weakness look like strength, our sentiment like love, our cowardice like courage . . .**

Stand firm like a rock. Truth always triumphs.

# Search for Spiritualism

There were two things that made Narendranath remarkable as a child. One was his endless questioning and the second was his ability to lose himself deeply in meditation. Though he was also naughty and restless, he was drawn to a certain kind of spiritualism even as a child. Like every Indian child, he listened to the stories from the epics, the Ramayana and the Mahabharata, and other folktales as well as other stories his mother told him. These left a deep impression on him. His father would also engage him in long conversations, about nature and the role of every being, plant and animal on the earth.

Naren loved playing at meditation—perhaps it wasn't playing, after all, as his life would show later. As a child, away from the other boisterous games he was fond of, he could be found at times sitting in quiet worship before the images of Rama, Sita or Shiva.

He knew verses from the epics, and could recite them by heart. Sometimes he would correct songs sung by the wandering bards who often appeared on their street and stopped by the house. He used to play with the *syce* or stable-hand by dressing up as a mendicant or *vairagi*, someone who had renounced worldly pleasures. He would dress in rags and smear himself with ashes. He was known to give away things without a second thought to anyone who stopped by asking for a morsel to eat or a few coins, and so Naren was locked up whenever a wandering sadhu was sighted down the street. It is said that every night just before falling asleep, he envisioned being bathed in a radiant white glow that appeared between his eyes. It left him feeling at peace.

He would never tire of listening to stories from the epics and as a young boy believed in them too. One day he went to hear a discourse on the Ramayana and the pundit described in flowery detail the story of the monkey god Hanuman and his devotion to Rama, the exiled prince of Ayodhya. At the end of it all, Naren asked the pundit if he could tell him where Hanuman could be found. The pundit, tired after a long session, tried to put Naren off by suggesting that he look for Hanuman in a nearby banana grove. Narendranath waited there late into at night, hoping he would indeed find Hanuman there. His family and friends found him only after a long search. Such was his perseverance in seeking what he sought!

Naren moved with his father and the rest of his family to Raipur for two years. It was a long journey. As they proceeded on a bullock cart through the dry forests, he saw far ahead, two tall hills and in a cleft between the hills, stretching from its bottom to the very crest, he noticed an intricate beehive crafted by bees working over a long period of time. It was a vision that transfixed him. The majesty of the mountains and the painstaking efforts of the tiny creatures made a profound impression and it is said he lost consciousness for a long moment.

When a granduncle of his lay dying, he called Naren to recite passages from the Mahabharata to him. The dying man was intensely moved at Naren's narration, especially at the part when Garuda, who as half-eagle, half-man serves as Vishnu's vehicle, flies away after having rescued his mother Vinata from his half-brothers who had enslaved her. It was a symbol of the soul rising with its new-found knowledge to a state of bliss.

To his friends at the Metropolitan Institute in Calcutta he would always say that his ambition was to be a sage. It was a time of change and there were opportunities, especially of serving the British government, but he was quite adamant and often played at being a sadhu with his friends. He would offer his palm and say that the lines on his hand indicated that he would lead the life of a wandering monk and whenever he heard stories of such monks he would be fascinated.

He was also influenced by his father, who was a generous, well-read man. Vishwanath Dutta believed all religions preached the same principles and he treated everyone he came across with the same kindness. Naren also learnt some spiritual lessons from his pet white mice, whom he kept in a small iron pen. The pen had wheels and the mice kept running over these, time and time again, oblivious to the fact that they could never get away. To Vivekananda, it spoke of the timelessness of the universe, and that everyone had simply to do his or her duty.

After college he wasn't quite sure of what to do. It was a time of great ferment and questioning. India was a colonized nation, but among the educated and the aware, there were efforts afoot to reform the country in many ways. Narendranath was sensitive to the events in these momentous times: he knew that despite the modern methods introduced by the British rule, the latter itself was in question, but he looked within for answers.

It was his search for spiritual meaning that led him to Shri Ramakrishna. He had heard of Shri Ramakrishna from various people, from his friends and even his principal, the Reverend William Hastie of the Scottish Church College. From his very youth, two visions of life presented themselves to him. He knew he could easily find himself a place among the city's elite, rich and powerful, and win for himself great wealth and honour too. On the other hand, he knew he also wanted to give up all worldly things and ambitions, and live simply and with few wants, a life that most sages he had read about, lived. It was a wish that consumed him and he longed to emulate such sages.

It was an age when there was intense questioning, a re-examining of old traditions and philosophies. Narendranath, having studied philosophy and history, was aware of the different streams of thought and he had many questions and few answers. He knew the western philosophical systems that stressed rationality and he was aware of the spiritual and mystical traditions he had grown up with and valued. He was interested in knowing who God really was and if God was a visible entity.

Besides the books recommended in his curriculum, he read other texts devoted to western philosophy and logic such as those by Herbert Spencer, Immanuel Kant and Schopenhauer. He learnt of the mystical and analytical speculation that Aristotle the Greek philosopher talked about, there was the positivist philosophy of Comte, and John Stuart Mill's *Three Essays on Religion*. He read history and also the nature poets like Percy Bysshe Shelley and William Wordsworth. He even read physiology hoping to understand how the nervous system worked.

There were things he found hard to reconcile. He had faith in what he had learnt from his mother, and yet reason and his argumentative nature meant he could not accept anything without evidence. His learning of the western texts, and speculation on illusion and reality only gave rise to more questions in his mind. Unable to find answers, he took to harsh austerities in the manner of sadhus and monks. Once at his maternal grandparents' house, he took to a strict diet, slept on bare, hard ground and used a thin quilt even when the nights were cold.

He followed the activities of the Brahmo Samaj, the social reform organization set up by the reformer Raja Ram Mohan Roy in 1830. The Brahmo Samaj stood for the abolition for various social evils such as *sati*, the custom of a widow burning herself on her husband's funeral pyre. The Samaj also encouraged education of women and widow remarriage, believing that even the ancient scriptures and texts sanctioned these. By the 1860s, however, the Brahmo Samaj had splintered into smaller groups, mainly due to differences between the generation of reformers who came after Roy. There was Debendranath Tagore's 'Tatvabodhini Samaj', and Keshub Chandra Sen's 'Brahmo Samaj of India'. They believed not in idolatry, but in monotheism, and continued to advocate the need for reform in Hindu society.

It was because Narendranath studied the texts of all religions that he realized that the foundations of all were the same. but he longed for spiritual illumination. If everyone was alike, why were there differences? He longed to find the ideal path. He went to Debendranath Tagore, and asked him if he had seen God. This question embarrassed Tagore and he advised Narendranath to 'practise meditation'. Narendranath was disappointed with his response, but he received no better answer from the leaders of other religious sects whom he approached with the same question.

At this critical juncture he remembered the words of his professor, William Hastie, who, while speaking of mystical trances in the course of his lectures, had mentioned Shri Ramakrishna. The class was discussing Wordsworth's poem, *The Excursion,* and Hastie explained that if a person was of mystical nature and pure in mind, he could experience such trances. He said: 'Such an experience is the result of purity of mind and concentration on some particular object, and is rare indeed, particularly in these days. I have seen only one person who has experienced that blessed state of mind, and he is Shri Ramakrishna Paramahamsa of Dakshineswar. You can understand if you go there and see for yourself.' The young seeker decided to try once more to find on answer to his question.

It was this that made him seek out Shri Ramakrishna and accept him as his teacher. Though Narendranath too was anointed as a monk by Shri Ramakrishna in 1886, spiritualism wasn't merely about meditating and living the life of a recluse. Shri Ramakrishna recognized the spirituality that united man (*Atman*) to a divine being (*Brahman*). This was the Advaita that Vivekananda thought and wrote about, the philosophy outlined in the Vedas and the Upanishads—collectively known as the Vedanta. It emphasized the divinity of every being but to Vivekananda, spirituality would soon come to encompass service to mankind for the latter symbolized a divine service.

Shri Ramakrishna died in 1886, and Vivekananda followed his guru's teachings and precepts diligently. However, in his search of what spiritualism meant, Vivekananda recognized great teachers of every religion, of all ages and learnt from them. After Shri Ramakrishna's death, and ensuring that the monastic order, the Ramakrishna Math, to continue his teacher's work was in a secure state, he decided to travel across India as a wandering monk. He carried his *kamandal* or the brass water vessel used by all monks, and two books, the Gita and *The Imitation of Christ* by Thomas à Kempis, a German monk who lived in the 14th century. In Allahabad he was moved on meeting a Muslim saint and called him like Shri Ramakrishna, a *paramahamsa*, a great soul. Next he went to Ghazipur where he came to know Pavhari Baba.

Pavhari Baba had studied many texts of Hindu philosophy. He lived an austere life as a sage by the banks of the Ganga at Ghazipur in the United Provinces, now Uttar Pradesh. He spent most of his time meditating, and lived on practically nothing and so people affectionately referred to him as the 'air-eating holy man'. No one could fail to be moved by Pavhari Baba's simplicity and goodness. There was a time he was bitten by a cobra and in the midst of terrible pain, he only said that the snake had been a form of his Beloved, for he considered the divine power as such. He lived on very little and would often give away his food to beggars and monks, and go hungry instead. Pavhari Baba held Shri Ramakrishna in high regard and kept in his bare room a picture of him. When he was not meditating, he would answer people's queries or console them from behind a wall. One day the sight of smoke from his room alerted people to the fact that he had set himself on fire, realizing his days were numbered. It was considered an act of sacrifice.

Naren would always remember two of his instructions. Pavhari Baba believed that the student should always serve and be humble towards his teacher. He also insisted that the means one adopted spiritually should matter as much as the goal.

As a wandering monk, Narendranath mingled with all kinds of people. He stayed in roadside huts, had meals with the poor and the downtrodden, and in contrast, was also accorded lavish hospitality when he was a guest of kings such as those who ruled over Khetri in Rajasthan, and Mysore and Ramnad in south India.

But the more he actually saw, and experienced, the more he was convinced of the core truths. A life of seclusion devotion to learning and meditation wasn't enough. Spiritualism was also different from the performance of miracles. A headman in a village up north was once believed to be possessed by strange spirits. The villagers came to him too. A heated axe was brought to the man but to his wonder, it did not scorch his hair or burn his skin at all. But when Vivekananda touched it, his fingers were singed. It puzzled him no end, he could not believe that the display and possession of such powers indicated a spiritually perfect being.

At the same time, he couldn't be merely a religious recluse, for he had to work for the good of the people, for on this path lay the mission of service and a true yearning for the divine. If the presence of the divine was obvious in every being, he asked, wouldn't giving one's life to serving every being, easing their pain and worries, be a spiritual journey in itself.

Narendranath's saw his spiritual voyage as a two-fold path. It wasn't merely enough to serve people, especially the poor and the suffering, but he had to spread this message, and the lessons of philosophy that ancient India had to offer to the western world. The latter, he saw, was rapidly modernizing, but materialism did not provide complete answers. His spiritual journey thus came to be an ambitious one. It comprised the need to ease suffering and to promote understanding among the world's people. The message of Vedanta, which proclaimed the divinity of the soul and the oneness of existence, could alone unite and heal the wounds of India and the world. It was this that made him seek an opportunity to speak of Hinduism and Vedanta philosophy at Chicago's Parliament of Religions in 1893. After this, Vivekananda became a popular figure in America because what he said and wrote about was accessible to all.

In the west, he would sometimes be annoyed if asked irritating questions. But he would not mock anyone's beliefs. He just asked them to see the divinity in themselves and in others. For three years he spread Vedanta philosophy in America and Europe. Every address of his began with references to the scriptures and he drew examples from every religion. For example in the US, after a short meditation, he opened with the Gospel according to Saint John, and also from the Bible. He taught from the Bhagavad Gita, the Upanishads, the Vedanta Sutras, the Bhakti Sutras of Narada, and other Hindu scriptures. He discussed Vedanta as developed by saint-philosophers such as Shankaracharya, Ramanuja and Madhavacharya. He also spoke at length about Shri Ramakrishna, of his own life with his teacher, and of his struggles with the tendency towards scepticism and agnosticism. He told stories from the epics and mythology to illustrate his deep and complex thoughts.

In his books, and lectures, he talked of the essential unity of all religions, the need for mindfulness, and the search within that would lead to God. He then returned to India in 1897 to found the Ramakrishna Mission. Those who dedicated themselves to the Ramakrishna Mission were to be workers in the service of God.

## What Swami Vivekananda Said

You have to grow from the inside out. None can teach you, none can make you spiritual. There is no other teacher but your own soul.

**Are you unselfish? That is the question. If you are, you will be perfect without reading a single religious book, without going into a single church or temple.**

Where can we go to find God if we cannot see Him in our own hearts and in every living being?

**Of one hundred persons who take up the spiritual life, eighty turn out to be charlatans, fifteen insane, and only five, maybe, get a glimpse of the real truth. Therefore, beware.**

As different streams having different sources all mingle their waters in the sea, so different tendencies, various though they appear, crooked or straight, all lead to God.

**All the powers in the universe are already ours. It is we who have put our hands before our eyes and cry that it is dark.**

Man is to become divine by realizing the divine. Idols or

temples, or churches or books, are only the supports, the help of his spiritual childhood.

**You cannot believe in God until you believe in yourself.**

After so much austerity I have known that the highest truth is this: He is present in every being! These are all in manifold forms of him. There is no other God to seek for! He alone is worshipping God, who serves all beings!

**This is the one central idea in the Gita: work incessantly, but be not attached to it.**

Can you see your own eyes? God is like that. He is as close as your own eyes. He is your own, even though you can't see Him.

**The world is the great gymnasium where we come to make ourselves strong.**

We never build anew, we simply change places; we cannot have anything new, we only change the position of things. The seed grows into the tree, patiently and gently; we must direct our energies towards the truth, and fulfil the truth that exists, not try to make new truths.

**The moment I have realized God sitting in the temple of every human body, the moment I stand in reverence before every human being and see God in him—that moment I am free from bondage, everything that binds vanishes, and I am free.**

Truth can be stated in a thousand different ways, yet each one can be true.

**As soon as you make a sect, you protest against universal brotherhood.**

It is good and very grand to conquer external nature, but grander still to conquer the internal nature of man. It is grand and good to know the laws that govern the stars and planets; it is infinitely grander and better to know the laws that govern the passions, the feelings, the will, of mankind. This conquering of the inner man, understanding the secrets of the subtle workings that are within the human mind, and knowing its wonderful secrets, belong entirely to religion.

**Each individual has to work out his own salvation; there is no other way, and so also with nations.**

There is no other teacher but your own soul.

**All differences in this world are of degree, and not of kind, because oneness is the secret of everything.**

God is to be worshipped as the one beloved, dearer than everything in this and next life.

**That man has reached immortality who is disturbed by nothing material.**

External nature is only internal nature writ large.

**When an idea exclusively occupies the mind, it is transformed into an actual physical or mental state.**

What the world wants is character. The world is in need of those whose life is one burning love, selfless. That love will make every word tell like a thunderbolt.

**When we come to non-attachment, then we can understand the marvellous mystery of the universe: how it is intense activity and at the same time intense peace, how it is work every moment and rest every moment.**

If faith in ourselves had been more extensively taught and practised, I am sure a very large portion of the evils and miseries that we have would have vanished.

Our duty is to encourage everyone in his struggle to live up to his own highest idea, and strive at the same time to make the ideal as near as possible to the Truth.

As different streams having different sources all mingle their waters in the sea, so different tendencies, various though they appear, crooked or straight, all lead to God.

The greatest truths are the simplest things in the world, simple as your own existence.

Feel nothing, know nothing, do nothing, have nothing, give up all to God, and say utterly, 'Thy will be done.' We only dream this bondage. Wake up and let it go.

As all the rivers of the world constantly pour their waters into the ocean, but the ocean's grand, majestic nature remains undisturbed and unchanged, so even though all the senses bring in sensations from nature, the ocean-like heart of the sage knows no disturbance, knows no fear.

Let miseries come in millions of rivers and happiness in hundreds! I am no slave to misery! I am no slave to happiness.

**The real individuality is that which never changes and will never change; and that is the God within us.**

. . . Try to be pure and unselfish—that is the whole of religion. The secret of religion lies not in theories but in practice. To be good and to do good—that is the whole of religion.

**My lady has furniture in her parlour, from all over the world, and now it is the fashion to have something Japanese; so she buys a vase and puts it in her room. Such is religion with the vast majority; they have all sorts of things for enjoyment, and unless they add a little flavour of religion, life is not all right, because society would criticise them. Society expects it; so they must have some religion. This is the present state of religion in the world.**

Who will help you? You are the help of the universe. What in this universe can help you? What can prevail over you? You are the God of the universe; where can you seek for help? Never help came from anywhere but from yourself.

**In your ignorance, every prayer that you made and that was answered, you thought was answered by some Being, but you answered the prayer yourself unknowingly.**

All who have actually attained any real religious experience, never wrangle over the form in which the different religions are expressed. They know that the soul of all religions is the same and so they have no quarrel with anybody just because he or she does not speak in the same tongue.

**The very reason for nature's existence is for the education of the soul**

In a conflict between the heart and the brain, follow your heart.

**The moment I have realized God sitting in the temple of every human body, the moment I stand in reverence before every human being and see God in him—that moment I am free from bondage, everything that binds vanishes, and I am free.**

There is no God separate from you, no God higher than you, the real 'you'. All the gods are little beings to you, all the ideas of God and Father in heaven are but your own reflection. God Himself is your image.

**'God created man after His own image.' That is wrong. Man creates God after his own image . . . Throughout the universe we are creating gods after our own image. We create the god and fall down**

**at his feet and worship him; and when this dream comes, we love it!**

This attachment of Love to God is indeed one that does not bind the soul but effectively breaks all its bondages

**God did not give me everything that I wanted. But, He gave me everything that I needed!**

Each soul is potentially divine. The goal is to manifest this divinity by controlling nature, external and internal. Do this either by work, or worship, or psychic control, or philosophy—by one, or more, or all of these—and be free. This is the whole of religion. Doctrines, or dogmas, or rituals, or books, or temples, or forms, are but secondary details.

**What philosophy insists on is not to give up joys, but to know what joy really is.**

Do you think you can teach even a child? You cannot. The child teaches himself. Your duty is to afford opportunities and to remove obstacles. A plant grows. Do you make the plant grow? Your duty is to put a hedge round it and see that no animal eats up the plant, and there your duty ends.

**After every happiness comes misery; they may be**

far apart or near. The more advanced the soul, the more quickly does one follow the other. What we want is neither happiness nor misery. Both make us forget our true nature; both are chains—one iron, one gold; behind both is the *Atman*, who knows neither happiness nor misery. These are states, and states must ever change; but the nature of the Atman is bliss, peace, unchanging. We have not to get it, we have it; only wash away the dross and see it.

When love to God is revealed and is all, this world appears like a drop.

The old religions said that he was an atheist who did not believe in God. The new religion says that he is an atheist who does not believe in himself.

# Shri Ramakrishna, the Teacher

**N**arendranath was curious right from childhood about the existence of God. By the time he reached college, he was vehement in his desire to know the truth about God. He had questioned holy people and scholars, asking them if they had seen God. He was disappointed in most of the answers he received.

Then he remembered having heard the name of Shri Ramakrishna Paramahamsa from the Reverend William Hastie, who while lecturing his class on Wordsworth's poem *The Excursion*, had spoken of people experiencing trances. Hastie had added that he only knew of Shri Ramakrishna, the priest of the Kali temple at Dakshineswar in Calcutta, who was a true saint and had had such experiences.

Narendranath had also heard about Shri Ramakrishna from a relative, Ramachandra Datta, who was a 'householder disciple' of Shri Ramakrishna and thus different from those disciples who had renounced the world. When he heard of Naren's unwillingness to marry and his desire to lead a spiritual life, Ramachandra had suggested that he meet Shri Ramakrishna at Dakshineswar.

Shri Ramakrishna was born to a family of priests, and since childhood had numerous mystical experiences. It was his older brother Ramkumar who was first the priest of the temple that was built by Rani Rashmoni in 1855. She was from the caste of the

Kaivartas, and so was looked down on by the orthodox. Following Ramkumar's early death, Shri Ramakrishna became the temple priest. Shri Ramakrishna had been exposed to a lot of spiritual and religious influences since childhood, and was aware of the many strands within Hinduism, and the essential tenets of other religions such as Islam and Christianity. To him all religions were different means of reaching God.

Narendranath was already popular as a good singer. It was at the house of Surendranath Mitra, another disciple of Shri Ramakrishna, that the latter first heard Narendranath sing.

The next time they met was when Narendranath, curious about all that he had heard about Shri Ramakrishna, went to Dakshineswar with the same question about God. This time he would be surprised by his answer.

Approaching Shri Ramakrishna, Narendranath asked him the question he had asked others before: 'Have you seen God?'

With no hesitation, Shri Ramakrishna replied that he had, he could see God just as clearly as he saw Naren in front of him, and that he saw god in a more 'intense sense'. He went on to clarify that the presence of the Divine could indeed be experienced or felt if the wish for this was heartfelt, but no one really bothered, for everyone was too wrapped up in their own lives. But if one really sought God with all one's desire for Him, divinity would make itself apparent everywhere; as Shri Ramakrishna said in words used by Vivekananda in his book on his teacher, titled *My Master*: 'One can see and talk to Him as I am doing with you. But who cares to do so? People shed torrents of tears for their wife and children, for wealth and property, but who does so for the sake of God? If one weeps sincerely for Him. He surely manifests Himself.'

This unexpected reply impressed Narendranath. For the first time he had found someone who could say that he had seen God, and recognized that religion was not something distant or even a necessary chore but a reality to be absorbed and felt. As he listened, he could not but believe that Shri Ramakrishna spoke from the depths of his own learning and experiences. However, he still nursed his doubts.

There were other pressures on him, too.

He was then only 21 and had just lost his father. It was a difficult time for his family and Naren, being the oldest, had yet to make any permanent arrangements for his mother and siblings. So it crossed his mind to request Thakur—as Shri Ramakrishna was popularly called—to put in a prayer to the deity he worshipped so that his mother and siblings could be well rid of their hardships.

However, Shri Ramakrishna refused his request, saying he had never asked the Goddess Kali for anything. If he so wanted, Naren could pray for himself at the auspicious hour. But when Naren did so, and entered the shrine as directed by Shri Ramakrishna, he forgot what he had come to ask for. Instead he asked for the ability to understand between what was right and wrong, and the quality of detachment, spiritual knowledge and undying devotion. On his return, he sheepishly admitted to Thakur what had happened, and on the latter's advice, tried again. This happened at least twice and at last Naren realized the folly of what he was doing. It was like asking for an ordinary 'gourd', a common garden vegetable, from the king when he could have all the riches he wanted.

There had been other meetings too, when Narendranath would lose himself in a higher spiritual world while meditating. Shri Ramakrishna knew he had found the ideal disciple in him. Shri Ramakrishna was mystical and had deep spiritual insights that were not easily explained, and Narendranath became his most devoted and cherished disciple.

Narendranath understood that a teacher was not just someone who taught, but who adopted his disciples like a parent. Once when Narendranath was very sick, Shri Ramakrishna was beset with worry and walked several miles to where he was recuperating at a friend's house.

Often Narendranath used to tease Shri Ramakrishna for his devotion, telling him the mythological story of the king Bharata who was so devoted to his pet deer that he would worry and think of the deer constantly, even when he was dying. His love and concern, the story went, caused him to be born as a deer in his next life. Shri Ramakrishna would give Naren books to read such as the *Ashtavakra Samhita* (a dialogue between the sage Ashtavakra and the king Janaka of Mithila), the Bhagavad Gita, some of the Puranas and even the *Adhyatma Ramayana*, an old Sanskrit text that talked of the many values of the prince Rama and is believed to have been originally written by the sage Vyasa, in the form of a conversation between Shiva and his consort, the Goddess Parvati.

On another occasion, Shri Ramakrishna asked Naren to read a book that purported to accurately forecast the rainfall expected to occur that year. After he was done, Shri Ramakrishna asked him to squeeze its pages, but not a drop of water emerged, of course. Books on religion, Shri Ramakrishna explained, claimed to really explain God, but such books were of little use. It was all to be experienced. From Shri Ramakrishna, Narendranath learnt that all religions are not contradictory or antagonistic. They are but various phases of one eternal religion.

Shri Ramakrishna never spoke a harsh word to anyone and was quietly tolerant. When he was called mad to his face, he would reply that everyone was mad after something, so it was best he was mad in his adoration for the Divine.

One day Naren complained to his teacher that he could not meditate in the morning as the piercing whistle from a mill in his neighbourhood bothered him. Shri Ramakrishna suggested that if he concentrated on the very sound of the whistle, he would overcome the distraction in no time.

Naren would also argue with Shri Ramakrishna, but his teacher never forbade him to do anything or forced him to accept his teachings blindly. Of all the disciples of Shri Ramakrishna, Narendranath alone doubted him on occasion and criticized those of his teachings that appeared irrational to him. Shri Ramakrishna would encourage Naren to question him always, to test him in the same way that moneychangers checked their coins. He was not to accept anything his teacher said until he was thoroughly convinced of it. Shri Ramakrishna allayed several of his doubts, but he also gave him the freedom and confidence to seek his own truths.

Narendranath was, in the beginning, sceptical of the doctrine of Advaita Vedanta that Shri Ramakrishna believed in. The Advaita idea in ancient philosophy believed that the identity of the individual soul was alike in every way to the 'Supreme Self' or what was called God, and this appeared to him quite blasphemous. To Shri Ramakrishna this was what the search for truth was all about, and he tried his best to explain this to Naren by reason and argument, but for long met with little success. But once Naren, in a meditative state, experienced this feeling of oneness with everything around him, and he understood what Shri Ramakrishna was trying to say. Everything in the universe appeared united in a fundamental way; everything, after all, was created from the same material, so there was a certain unity to all things in the universe.

His teacher was pleased with Naren's spiritual search and his questioning mind. He made no secret of his wish to make him his spiritual heir. Once Shri Ramakrishna realized that he was sick, he also wanted Naren to look after the young disciples. Shri Ramakrishna passed on in 1886 after a long illness and he left his other disciples in Naren's care.

Despite the advice of all physicians who saw him, Shri Ramakrishna continued to guide all spiritual seekers who came to him and his students. To ensure he had the best possible care, he was first looked after by his disciples in a house in the northern section of Calcutta and then to a garden house at Cossipore, a Calcutta suburb. Naren and his other disciples took charge of nursing him. By 1886, Shri Ramakrishna had already initiated several of his disciples into the monastic life, and this was how the future Ramakrishna order of monks or the Ramakrishna Math started.

After Shri Ramakrishna's death, Naren, as a *sanyasi*, did not hesitate to take on the hardships and difficulties this life involved.

His other disciples continued to follow his teachings, often rising at three in the morning to begin their prayers and meditation. Narendranath's family remained in dire straits in these years. His two brothers were still studying and till 1889 circumstances were indeed difficult. Naren would sometimes feel himself weak and bereft of all strength, but he had a vision now, a spiritual goal to work towards.

Soon after his teacher's death, one of his wealthier disciples bought an abandoned house at Baranagore near Calcutta for Shri Ramakrishna's disciples and the monks Shri Ramakrishna had initiated. But they just about managed to survive those initial years. The house was rumoured to be haunted, and they were without funds to even sustain themselves. Sometimes there was very little food, just rice and salt. His disciples, however, did not give in. They begged, they travelled long distances and carried out welfare work wherever it was needed, such as during famines.

Shri Ramakrishna is referred to as Paramahamsa, which means 'a great soul'. An annual event in Belur, where Vivekananda set up the Ramakrishna Math in his teacher's honour, marks the occasion of Shri Ramakrishna's death.

It was Vivekananda who in a few years' time carried his teacher's message to the world, about the need to find God in oneself, and to see the essential harmony in all things and all religions. However, Vivekananda differed in his belief and practice, which linked the worship and service of God to the service of mankind and all creatures. It was with this thought that he founded the Ramakrishna Mission, which continues to spread the message of spirituality, seeks to promote understanding among religions and engages in humanitarian and welfare work across India and in various countries.

Later he wrote of his teacher:

> This man came to live near Calcutta, the capital of India, the most important university town in our country, which was sending out sceptics and materialists by the hundreds every year. Yet many of these university men—sceptics and agnostics—used to come and listen to him. I heard of this man, and I went to hear him. He looked just like an ordinary man, with nothing remarkable about him. He used the most simple language, and I thought, 'Can this man be a great teacher?'—crept near to him and asked him the question which I had been asking others all my life: 'Do you believe in God, Sir?'
>
> 'Yes,' he replied.
>
> 'Can you prove it, Sir?'
>
> 'Yes.'
>
> 'How?'
>
> 'Because I see Him just as I see you here, only in a much intenser sense.'
>
> That impressed me at once. For the first time I found a man who dared to say that he saw God that religion was a reality to be felt, to be sensed in an infinitely more intense way than we can sense the world. I began to go to that man, day after day, and I actually saw that religion could be given.

# What Swami Vivekananda Said

Shri Ramakrishna use to say, 'As long as I live, so long do I learn. That man or that society which has nothing to learn is already in the jaws of death.'

**How often does a man ruin his disciples by remaining always with them! When men are once trained, it is essential that their leader leave them, for without his absence they cannot develop themselves. Plants always remain small under a big tree.**

My Master taught me this lesson hundreds of times, yet I often forget it. Few understand the power of thought. If a man goes into a cave, shuts himself in, and thinks one really great thought and dies, that thought will penetrate the walls of that cave, vibrate through space, and at last permeate the whole human race. Such is the power of thought; be in no hurry therefore to give your thoughts to others. First have something to give.

**He alone teaches who has something to give, for teaching is not talking, teaching is not imparting doctrines, it is communicating. Spirituality can be communicated just as really as I can give you a flower.**

. . . First make character—that is the highest duty you can perform.

**Know Truth for yourself, and there will be many to whom you can teach it after wards; they will all come. This was the attitude of my Master.**

He criticized no one. For years I lived with that man, but never did I hear those lips utter one word of condemnation for any sect. He had the same sympathy for all sects; he had found the harmony between them.

**A man may be intellectual, or devotional, or mystic, or active; the various religions represent one or the other of these types. Yet it is possible to combine all the four in one man, and this is what future humanity is going to do. That was his idea. He condemned no one, but saw the good in all.**

People came by thousands to see and hear this wonderful man who spoke in a patois every word of which was forceful and instinct with light. For it is not what is spoken, much less the language in which it is spoken, but it is the personality of the speaker which dwells in everything he says that carries weight. Every one of us feels this at times.

We hear most splendid orations, most wonderfully reasoned-out discourses, and we go home and forget them all. At other times we hear a few words in the simplest language, and they enter into our lives, become part and parcel of ourselves and produce lasting results.

All teaching implies giving and taking, the teacher gives and the taught receives, but the one must have something to give, and the other must be open to receive.

One touch, one glance, can change a whole life. I have read about Buddha and Christ and Mohammed, about all those different luminaries of ancient times, how they would stand up and say, 'Be thou whole', and the man became whole. I now found it to be true, and when I myself saw this man, all scepticism was brushed aside.

. . . My Master used to say, 'Religion can be given and taken more tangibly, more really than anything else in the world.' Be therefore spiritual first; have something to give and then stand before the world and give it. Religion is not talk, or doctrines, or theories; nor is it sectarianism. Religion cannot live in sects and societies. It is the relation between the soul and God; how can it be made into a society? It would then degenerate into business, and wherever there are business and business principles in religion, spirituality dies.

**Religion does not consist in erecting temples, or building churches, or attending public worship. It is not to be found in books, or in words, or in lectures, or in organizations. Religion consists in realization. As a fact, we all know that nothing will satisfy us until we know the truth for ourselves.**

One infinite religion existed all through eternity and will ever exist, and this religion is expressing itself in various countries in various ways. Therefore, we must respect all religions and we must try to accept them all as far as we can.

**Religions manifest themselves not only according to race and geographical position, but according to individual powers. In one man religion is manifesting itself as intense activity, as work. In another it is manifesting itself as intense devotion, in yet another, as mysticism, in others as philosophy, and so forth.**

It is wrong when we say to others, 'Your methods are not right.' Perhaps a man, whose nature is that of love, thinks that the man who does good to others is not on the right road to religion, because it is not his own way, and is, therefore, wrong. If the philosopher thinks, 'Oh, the poor ignorant people, what do they know about a God of Love, and loving Him? They do not know what they mean,' he is wrong, because they may be right and he also.

**To learn this central secret that the truth may be one and yet many at the same time, that we may have different visions of the same truth from different standpoints, is exactly what must be done. Then, instead of antagonism to anyone, we shall have infinite sympathy with all.**

Knowing that as long as there are different natures born in this world, the same religious truth will require different adaptations, we shall understand that we are bound to have forbearance with each other.

**The more such men are produced in a country, the more that country will be raised; and that country where such men absolutely do not exist is simply doomed nothing can save it.**

To proclaim and make clear the fundamental unity underlying all religions was the mission of my Master. Other teachers have taught special religions which bear their names, but this great teacher of the nineteenth century made no claim for himself. He left every religion undisturbed because he had realized that in reality they are all part and parcel of the one eternal religion.

**Do not accept anything because I have said so; but test everything for yourself. It is not in assent or dissent that the goal is to be attained, but in actual and concrete realization.**

This is the message of Shri Ramakrishna to the modern world: 'Do not care for doctrines, do not care for dogmas, or sects, or churches, or temples; they count for little compared with the essence of existence in each man which is spirituality; and the more this is developed in a man, the more powerful is he for good. Earn that first, acquire that, and criticise no one, for all doctrines and creeds have some good in them. Show by your lives that religion does not mean words, or names, or sects, but that it means spiritual realization. Only those can understand who have felt. Only those who have attained spirituality can communicate it to others, can be great teachers of mankind. They alone are the powers of light.'

# Serving the Nation

n 1890, four years after Shri Ramakrishna's death, Narendranath set off on his travels. Earlier he had made brief visits to places considered holy, such as Gaya and Varanasi, but had always returned to his fellow monks. Now he decided to set out on his own. His wanderings would be in two phases: to find things out for himself and to be alone; and then later when he branched out to different countries, it was to arouse awareness about India's heritage and its present, and to find people who could work for regenerating India.

When he left Calcutta in 1890, it was with the determination never to return. He had decided first to go to the Himalayas and lose himself in meditation and in his own spiritual thoughts. He went away, his heart filled with the desire to be an anonymous wandering monk, with only a staff and begging-bowl in hand and two books, the Gita and *The Imitation of Christ*. He warned his fellow monks not to go in search of him. Narendranath left on a journey of learning and rediscovery, and it would be a revelation in many ways. When they would finally get news of him, it was three years later when newspapers in India too mentioned his historic address at the Parliament of World Religions in Chicago.

He went to Varanasi, one of India's holiest places, where he met the well-known Vedic scholar Pramadadas Mitra. They would exchange a long correspondence over the next few years, discussing several aspects of the Hindu scriptures. From Varanasi, he went north to Ayodhya and Lucknow, then on to Agra and Vrindavan. These were places famous in history and in tradition. He often changed his name to avoid recognition. In January 1891, Naren set out for Delhi, assuming the name of Swami Vividishananda. Its past glory made him once again understand the impermanence of material achievements.

During these days he both learnt and taught. He mixed with all—there were nights he was offered hospitality by the poor and the underprivileged. Then again, he also was the guest of maharajas, prime ministers, orthodox pundit and liberal college professors. He became aware of the people's joys and sorrows, hopes and frustrations. He witnessed the tragedies of the country and also thought about possible remedies. In the course of his travels Naren came to know how he must work to serve the people.

From Delhi, he turned westward, towards Rajputana, with its princely states ruled by maharajas. He stayed in Alwar, and Jaipur and then moved to Ajmer, renowned for the mausoleum of a renowned Sufi saint, Khwaja Moinuddin Chishti. At Mount Abu he visited the Jain temple of Dilwara. It was at Mount Abu that he met the Maharaja of Khetri, Ajit Singh Bahadur of the Shekhawat dynasty, who was soon to become one of his devoted disciples. It was the Raja of Khetri who later arranged for his travel to America in 1893 and also suggested the name Vivekananda for him.

He walked most of the way, not resting or stopping much. He was once travelling in the Himalayan region and the road stretched long and hard before him. He was in the company of other monks and one among them was soon exhausted and about to give up. It was then that Vivekananda told him to look down at his feet. There were many roads already crossed, he pointed out in encouragement, and what lay ahead would soon be traversed too: Everything was possible if one proceeded with strength, courage and with thoughts of the divine in oneself, he said.

He walked to Gujarat and Kathiawar in western India. At the princely state of Porbandar, he spent several months and learnt much in the company of its administrator and prime minister, Sankar Pandurang Pandit. He had an impressive library and had published and edited several ancient works such as the *Atharvaveda* and Kalidasa's *Raghuvamsa*. It was Pandit who, impressed greatly by Narendranath's erudition, advised him to travel west, to acquaint the western people with his enlightening interpretation of Hindu philosophy.

Narendranath moved to Baroda (now Vadodara), and then to Khandwa in central India, before he turned westward again, toward Bombay, Poona (now Mumbai and Pune), and Kolhapur. Following this, he visited the southern parts of the country, past Belgaum to Mysore and then towards Malabar. Often walking for long hours and for long distances in a day, he would be tired. It was on his way along the Konkan coast on foot that he saw a mirage: a shady grove and a welcoming lake. He was exhausted from the long journey and the vision shimmered, sometimes vanished and appeared again. He realized that this, like all tricks of the light and one's imagination, was just a distraction. He compared it to life and its many distractions and how important it was to do one's karma, one's duty.

At Mysore, he addressed a gathering of scholars and was praised for his understanding of the Vedanta. He also surprised a visiting Austrian musician at the king's palace with his knowledge of western music. He discussed with the maharaja his plan of going to America, but when the latter came forward with an offer to pay his expenses for the trip, he decided to make a final decision only after visiting the holy temple of Rameswaram.

From the picturesque Malabar coast, he stopped at Cape Comorin (now Kanyakumari) and from there he moved up to Rameswaram. At Rameswaram he met Bhaskara Setupati, the Raja of Ramnad, who later became one of his devoted disciples.

His experiences all through his travels made him aware of the prevailing conditions in India, and how suppressed its people were under colonial rule. He also realized that Indians had to work to end their own misery and poverty. He discussed with the Raja of Ramnad several of his ideas about education and improving conditions in agriculture so that the country would no longer be plagued by famines. The Raja too urged Vivekananda to represent India at the Parliament of Religions in Chicago and promised to help him in this venture. In Madras, enthusiastic young followers collected funds to help Vivekananda begin his work in India in an organized manner.

All through this itinerant life he exchanged ideas with people from all walks of life. He impressed everyone with his learning, gentleness, and vast knowledge of Indian and western cultures. Many of the ideas he expressed at this time were later repeated in his public lectures in America and India. One day it occurred to him that he had no right to lead the life of a wandering monk, or to beg for food from door to door. He believed he was thus depriving the poor of the few morsels that they could otherwise share with their families. With this thought he entered a forest and walked the whole day through it, till nightfall when he finally sat down under a tree, footsore and hungry. It was then in this tired and fatigued state that he saw a tiger approaching. He sat there calmly, but the tiger changed its mind and went off in another direction. Vivekananda spent that night in the forest, meditating on God's strange ways. In the morning he felt a new surge of power.

In a certain town in Rajputana, he was kept busy for three days and nights by people who came to him for advice and instruction. He had little time for his meals or to snatch a few minutes' rest. It was late when everyone had left and it was then that a poor man hesitatingly offered him some food. He apologized to Vivekananda for his offerings of grain and vegetables, saying he could not cook it for him for he was of a lower caste and tradition did not allow this. But Vivekananda persuaded him to prepare a meal for him. In central India, he also spent a few days with a family of sweepers who were considered outcasts, and forced to live outside the city precincts.

At Cape Comorin, he worshipped at the temple of the Goddess Durga, known here as Devi or Bhagwati. Then he swam 500 metres or so, off the mainland at Vavathurai. He headed towards a rock that rose high over the surging waves and spent some hours in meditation there. That rock where he meditated bears Vivekananda's name and, in 1970, the Vivekananda Rock Memorial was built here. The memorial has the Vivekananda Mandapam, with a statue of

Vivekananda, and the Shripada Mandapam. There is a meditation hall called the 'Dhyana Mandapam' next to the memorial. The merging of the three seas on three sides of the Indian Peninsula, the—Bay of Bengal to the east, the Arabian Sea on the west and the Indian Ocean in the south—can be seen from the Vivekananda Rock and Memorial.

On looking back after the completion of his long journey, Vivekananda realized that there was no greater work than seeking to alleviate the pitiable conditions in which most Indian people lived. They were at the mercy of their rulers, the landlords, and even the priests who exploited them in the name of tradition. He realized that India had to rejuvenate herself on her own. No imitation of the west would do. In the princely states, that made up one-fifth of India, he hoped the rulers would introduce social reforms, improve methods of education, and step up measures for the benefit of the people. He knew there had to be organized efforts to improve the lives of the poor and ignorant villagers, including sanitary conditions, methods of agriculture, and even the provision of clean water.

As a *sanyasi*, he had taken the vow to dedicate himself to the service of God; but this God, he was convinced, was revealed through humanity. And his own service to this God must begin, therefore, with the people of India. He had to inspire and work with young people and enthuse them to work for the good and advancement of the country.

One day a young man complained to Vivekananda that he could make little progress in spiritual life. He had worshipped at temples, and had tried rigorous meditation too, all at the behest of teachers

# What Swami Vivekananda Said

The more we come out and do good to others, the more our hearts will be purified, and God will be in them.

**The Land where humanity has attained its highest towards gentleness, towards generosity, towards purity, towards calmness—it is India.**

Our duty is to encourage everyone in his struggle to live up to his own highest idea, and strive at the same time to make the ideal as near as possible to the Truth.

**If money helps a man to do good to others, it is of some value; but if not, it is simply a mass of evil, and the sooner it is got rid of, the better.**

Condemn none: if you can stretch out a helping hand, do so. If you cannot, fold your hands, bless your brothers, and let them go their own way.

**What is now wanted is a combination of the greatest heart with the highest intellectuality, of infinite love with infinite knowledge.**

They alone live, who live for others.

**Have faith in Man, whether he appears to you to be a very learned one or a most ignorant one.**

The great secret of true success, of true happiness, is this: the man or woman who asks for no return, the perfectly unselfish person, is the most successful.

**Give up the idea that by ruling over others, you can do any good to them. But you can do just as much as you can in the case of the plant: you can supply the growing seed with the materials for the making up of its body, bringing to it the earth, the water, the air, that it wants. It will take all that it wants by its own nature, it will assimilate and grow by its own nature.**

By doing well the duty which is nearest to us, the duty which is in our hands, we make ourselves stronger.

**Now is wanted intense Karma-Yoga with unbounded courage and indomitable strength in the heart. Then only will the people of the country be roused.**

If in this hell of a world one can bring a little joy and peace even for a day into the heart of a single person, that much alone is true . . .

A few heart-whole, sincere, and energetic men and women can do more in a year than a mob in a century.

Be grateful to the man you help, think of him as God. Is it not a great privilege to be allowed to worship God by helping our fellow men?

Give up all those old discussions, old fights about things which are meaningless, which are nonsensical in their very nature. Think of the last six hundred or seven hundred years of degradation when grown-up men by hundreds have been discussing for years whether we should drink a glass of water with the right hand or the left, whether the hand should be washed three times or four times, whether we should gargle five or six times. What can you expect from men who pass their lives in discussing such momentous questions as these and writing most learned philosophies on them!

We are neither Vedantists, most of us now, nor Pauranics, nor Tantrics. We are just 'Don't-touchists'. Our religion is in the kitchen. Our God is the cooking-pot, and our religion is, 'Don't touch me, I am holy'. If this goes on for another century, every one of us will be in a lunatic asylum.

It is a sure sign of softening of the brain when the mind cannot grasp the higher problems of life; all originality is lost, the mind has lost all its strength, its activity, and its power of thought, and just tries to go round and round the smallest curve it can find.

Ask nothing; want nothing in return. Give what you have to give; it will come back to you—but do not think of that now, it will come back multiplied a thousandfold—but the attention must not be on that. Yet have the power to give: give, and there it ends. Learn that the whole of life is giving, that nature will force you to give. So give willingly.

Every moment of goodness and real life that we enjoy is when we do not think of ourselves.

Things do not grow better. They remain as they are; and we grow better by the changes we make in them.

It is because we dare not give, because we are not resigned enough to accede to this grand demand of nature, that we are miserable. The forest is gone, but we get heat in return. The sun is taking up water from the ocean, to return it in showers. You are a machine for taking and giving: you take, in order to give.

Ask, therefore, nothing in return; but the more you give, the more will come to you. The quicker you can empty the air out of this room, the quicker it will be filled up by the external air; and if you close all the doors and every aperture, that which is within will remain, but that which is outside will never come in, and that which is within will stagnate, degenerate, and become poisoned.

**A river is continually emptying itself into the ocean and is continually filling up again. Bar not the exit into the ocean. The moment you do that, death seizes you.**

Three things are necessary to make every man great, every nation great:
1. Conviction of the powers of goodness.
2. Absence of jealousy and suspicion.
3. Helping all who are trying to be and do good.

# Vivekananda, the writer

I t was on the eve of his departure to the US that Ajit Singh, the Raja of Khetri, gave him the name of Vivekananda, which stands for 'wisdom' (*vivek*) and 'bliss' (*ananda*). Relatively unknown until then, he leapt into fame at the Parliament of Religions held in Chicago in 1893, at which he spoke about Hinduism, and the Vedanta philosophy. His speech drew loud applause and was widely reported in the media.

His vast knowledge of eastern and western branches of philosophy, and his deep insights, eloquence, and ability to strike an empathetic chord with the audience made him a popular speaker. Soon, he was travelling to other cities in America to deliver lectures at which huge audiences gathered. He pleaded persuasively for a better understanding between India and the 'New World' to create a healthy synthesis between East and West, in all spheres from religion to science.

In spite of his busy schedule and a life of wandering and even hardships, Vivekananda wrote a great deal. There were not just his lectures but also the many letters he penned, to friends, disciples, well-wishers and his family. Between 1893 and 1902, when he passed away at the young age of thirty-nine, he wrote four books that were philosophical treatises, laying stress on the different ways to seek spirituality: *Jnana Yoga*, *Bhakti Yoga*, *Karma Yoga* and *Raja Yoga*.

More works appeared after his lifetime and today Vivekananda's collected works stand at nine volumes, containing all aspects of his written works.

The books he wrote are treatises on Hindu philosophy but in no way are they perplexing. They are lucidly written, peppered with stories and advice on how to practically implement all that the scriptures said. Swami Vivekananda once spoke of himself as a 'condensed India,' for he wished to explain India, its cultural traditions and philosophies to a west that was largely ignorant of it.

Some of his disciples too wrote about him, including Sister Nivedita who accompanied him on some of his travels in India. But it was Josiah Goodwin, who served as his dedicated stenographer and follower between the years 1895 to 1898 and helped to archive Vivekananda's speeches and writings.

Goodwin was only 25 when he replied to an advertisement placed in two New York city newspapers, *The Herald* and *The World* in December 1895. Some of Vivekananda's followers had applied for a stenographer to record his lectures. Goodwin was originally from England but had travelled to Australia before coming to America. Goodwin applied out of curiosity but soon became a devoted disciple of Vivekananda. He was a master stenographer who could keep up with him as well as grasp the spiritual content of all that he said.

Goodwin worked at a salary far below his commercial worth, saying it was a privilege for him to be associated with Vivekananda. He recorded many of Vivekananda's lectures in America and England. He was more than a stenographer and sometimes doubled up as a full-time personal assistant who managed Vivekananda's itinerary and day to day needs.

The first of Vivekananda's works, *Karma Yoga* was published in 1894. In it Vivekananda emphasized the value of work, for work was one's duty and work was what gave life meaning. He also talked of the need for a balance between inertia and work.

In *Bhakti Yoga*, Vivekananda wrote about the need for an undying devotion to God, and cited the works of the 11th century philosopher Ramanuja. He also quoted from the *Sermon on the Mount*.

In *Raja Yoga*, he spoke of the divinity of the soul, and dwelled extensively on the philosophy of Patanjali, an ancient scholar who lived around the 4th century CE. The book talks of the quality of mindfulness and the power of one's own mind. It contains a translation of Patanjali's Yoga maxims to which Vivekananda added his own explanations. Patanjali expounded, through these aphorisms, the philosophy of Yoga, the power of concentration and the quality of mindfulness that would, with practice, help in the attainment of spiritual perfection.

He dictated *Raja Yoga* to one of his disciples—S. Ellen Waldo of Brooklyn in New York. She would later describe the manner in which he had done so. There would be moments when he would be lost deep in thought and it would appear to her that he was meditating, totally oblivious to the task on hand. She would wait, her pen dipped in ink, unsure and uncertain. Then with no warning, he would begin talking again, lucidly and eloquently, carrying on just where he had broken off.

In *Jnana Yoga*, Vivekananda wrote of the wisdom necessary to experience god. He highlighted the main religious tendencies—

finding God through doing good work or charitable activities; by practising meditation in solitude, or by doing devotional acts before a deity.

His works received marked attention from several thinkers and scholars. When *Raja Yoga* was completed sometime around June 1895, it drew the attention of the Harvard philosopher William James. It was later to rouse the enthusiasm of Leo Tolstoy, the Russian novelist and philosopher. It was this that made James call Vivekananda the 'paragon of Vedantists.'

Max Müller and Paul Deussen, the famous European scholars of Indian thought and religion of the 19th century, held Swami Vivekananda in genuine respect and affection. The French philosopher Romain Rolland compared his eloquence and his use of words to the majestic works of great musicians like Beethoven and Handel, which never failed to move any listener.

On 25 March 1896, Vivekananda delivered his famous lecture on 'The Philosophy of Vedanta' before the students of the philosophy department of Harvard University. He discussed the fundamental aspects of Hinduism, explained the basis of caste to them, and talked of Christianity and Buddhism as well. It produced such an impression that he was offered the Chair of Eastern Philosophy in the university. Later a similar offer came from Columbia University, but he turned down both these offers for his life lay in is country, serving his countrymen.

It was his keen desire to write more and explain the apparently contradictory passages of the Upanishads. While in the USA, he asked his devotees in India to send him several texts including the

Upanishads, the Vedanta Sutras with their commentaries written by the leading scholars, and also the Brahmana portions of the Vedas, and the Puranas. He wanted to call this work *Maximum Testamentum*, for he hoped to translate and explain all these for the western reader. He wanted to make philosophy, always considered far too abstract, a subject that could have practical implications.

Rabindranath Tagore who was only two years older and Vivekananda's contemporary once suggested that everyone should read Vivekananda, for this would help secure a comprehensive understanding of India.

Tagore wrote about him thus: 'Vivekananda said that there was the power of God in every man, that God wanted to have our service through the poor. This is what I call real gospel. This gospel showed the path of infinite freedom from man's tiny egocentric self beyond the limits of all selfishness. This was no sermon relating to a particular ritual, nor was it a narrow injunction to be imposed upon one's external life. Vivekananda's gospel marked the awakening of man in his fullness... If you want to know India, study Vivekananda.'

# What Swami Vivekananda Said

The help which tends to make us spiritually strong is the highest help, next to it comes intellectual help and after that comes physical help.

**One idea comes out of all this—the condemnation of all weakness. This is a particular idea in all our teachings which I like, either in philosophy, or in religion, or in work. If you read the Vedas, you will find this word always repeated—fearlessness— fear nothing.**

Fear is a sign of weakness. A man must go about his duties without taking notice of the sneers and the ridicule of the world. If a man retires from the world to worship God, he must not think that those who live in the world and work for the good of the world are not worshipping God: neither must those who live in the world, for wife and children, think that those who give up the world are low vagabonds. Each is great in his own place.

**Pleasure is not the goal of man, but knowledge.**

Good and evil have an equal share in moulding character, and in some instances misery is a greater teacher than happiness. In studying the great characters the world has produced, I dare say, in the vast majority of cases, it would be found that it was misery that taught more than happiness, it was poverty that taught more than wealth, it was blows that brought out their inner fire more than praise.

**Now this knowledge, again, is inherent in man. No knowledge comes from outside; it is all inside.**

If you really want to judge the character of a man, look not at his great performances. Every fool may become a hero at one time or another. Watch a man do his most common actions; those are indeed the things which will tell you the real character of a great man.

**Great occasions rouse even the lowest of human beings to some kind of greatness, but he alone is the really great man whose character is great always, the same wherever he be.**

The men of mighty will the world has produced have all been tremendous workers—gigantic souls, with wills powerful enough to overturn worlds, wills they got by persistent work, through ages, and ages.

**No one can get anything unless he earns it.**

We are responsible for what we are; and whatever we wish ourselves to be, we have the power to make ourselves.

**Work for work's sake. There are some who are really the salt of the earth in every country and who work for work's sake, who do not care for name, or fame, or even to go to heaven. They work just because good will come of it. There are others who do good to the poor and help mankind from still higher motives, because they believe in doing good and love good.**

The motive for name and fame seldom brings immediate results, as a rule.

**If a man works without any selfish motive in view, does he not gain anything? Yes, he gains the highest. Unselfishness is more paying, only people have not the patience to practise it . . .**

A man who can work for five days, or even for five minutes, without any selfish motive whatever, without thinking of future, of heaven, of punishment, or anything of the kind, has in him the capacity to become a powerful moral giant. It is hard to do it, but in the heart of our hearts we know its value, and the good it brings.

**If you wish to help a man, never think what that man's attitude should be towards you. If you want to do a great or a good work, do not trouble to think what the result will be . . .**

The ideal man is he who, in the midst of the greatest silence and solitude, finds the intensest activity, and in the midst of the intensest activity finds the silence and solitude of the desert . . . He goes through the streets of a big city with all its traffic, and his mind is as calm as if he were in a cave, where not a sound could reach him; and he is intensely working all the time. That is the ideal of Karma Yoga.

**The gift of knowledge is a far higher gift than that of food and clothes; it is even higher than giving life to a man, because the real life of man consists of knowledge. Ignorance is death, knowledge is life.**

Ignorance is the mother of all the evil and all the misery we see.

**The older we grow, the longer we are knocked about in the world, the more callous we become; and we are apt to neglect things that even happen persistently and prominently around us.**

Look at the power of the word! There is a woman weeping and miserable; another woman comes along and speaks to her a few gentle words, the doubled up frame of the weeping woman becomes straightened at once, her sorrow is gone and she already begins to smile. Think of the power of words!

**Let us give up all this foolish talk of doing good to the world. It is not waiting for your or my help; yet we must work and constantly do good, because it is a blessing to ourselves. That is the only way we can become perfect.**

We ought not to hate anyone. This world will always continue to be a mixture of good and evil. Our duty is to sympathise with the weak and to love even the wrongdoer.

**It is a very hard thing to understand, but you will come to learn in time that nothing in the universe has power over you until you allow it to exercise such a power.**

Take risks in your life. If you win, you can lead. If you lose, you can guide.

**All our knowledge is based upon experience.**

Attachment is that which dwells on pleasure.

**The great king Yudhishthira once said that the most wonderful thing in life is that every moment we see people dying around us, and yet we think we shall never die. Surrounded by fools on every side, we think we are the only exceptions, the only learned men. Surrounded by all sorts of experiences of fickleness, we think our love is the only lasting love.**

Take up one idea. Make that one idea your life; dream of it; think of it; live on that idea. Let the brain, the body, muscles, nerves, every part of your body be full of that idea, and just leave every other idea alone. This is the way to success, and this is the way great spiritual giants are produced.

**There are in every country only a few hundreds who can be, and will be religious. The others cannot be religious, because they will not be awakened, and they do not want to be. The chief thing is to want God.**

The first of everything should go to the poor; we have only a right to what remains. The poor are God's representatives; anyone who suffers is His representative.

One portion of the food cooked in a household belongs to the animals also. They should be given food every day; there ought to be hospitals in every city in this country for poor, lame, or blind horses, cows, dogs, and cats, where they should be fed and taken care of.

Despondency is not religion, whatever else it may be. By being pleasant always and smiling, it takes you nearer to God, nearer than any prayer.

How can those minds that are gloomy and dull love? If they talk of love, it is false; they want to hurt others. Think of the fanatics; they make the longest faces, and all their religion is to fight against others in word and act . . . So the man who always feels miserable will never come to God.

It is not religion, it is diabolism to say, 'I am so miserable.' Every man has his own burden to bear. If you are miserable, try to be happy, try to conquer it.

People so often run from one extreme to the other. Let the mind be cheerful, but calm. Never let it run into excesses, because every excess will be followed by a reaction.

The first step is: What do we want? Let us ask ourselves this question every day: do we want God? You may read all the books in the universe, but this love is not to be had by the power of speech, not by the highest intellect, not by the study of various sciences.

**He who desires God will get Love, unto him God gives Himself. Love is always mutual, reflective.**

As the loving wife thinks of her departed husband, with the same love we must desire the Lord, and then we will find God, and all books and the various sciences would not be able to teach us anything.

**Now in intellectual development we can get much help from books, but in spiritual development, almost nothing. In studying books, sometimes we are deluded into thinking that we are being spiritually helped; but if we analyse ourselves, we shall find that only our intellect has been helped, and not the spirit.**

. . . Almost everyone of us can speak most wonderfully on spiritual subjects, but when the time of action comes, we find ourselves so woefully deficient. It is because books cannot give us that impulse from outside.

**We do not light a candle to see the sun. When the sun rises, we instinctively become aware of its**

**rising; and when a teacher of men comes to help us, the soul will instinctively know that it has found the truth.**

There are certain conditions necessary in the taught, and also in the teacher. The conditions necessary in the taught are purity, a real thirst after knowledge, and perseverance.

**No impure soul can be religious; that is the one great condition; purity in every way is absolutely necessary. The other condition is a real thirst after knowledge. Who wants? That is the question. We get whatever we want—that is an old, old law. He who wants, gets. To want religion is a very difficult thing, not as easy as we generally think.**

. . . We always forget that religion does not consist in hearing talks, or in reading books, but it is a continuous struggle, a grappling with our own nature, a continuous fight till the victory is achieved. It is not a question of one or two days, of years, or of lives, but it may be hundreds of lifetimes, and we must be ready for that. It may come immediately, or it may not come in hundreds of lifetimes; and we must be ready for that. The student who sets out with such a spirit finds success.

**It is all very well to talk of liberty and independence, but without humility, submission, veneration and faith, there will not be any religion.**

'The teacher must be wonderful, so also must be the taught,' says the Katha Upanishad.

**One man should not force another to worship what he worships. All attempts to herd together human beings by means of armies, force or arguments, to drive them pell-mell into the same enclosure and make them worship the same God have failed and will fail always, because it is constitutionally impossible to do so.**

You can take away the obstacles, but knowledge comes out of its own nature. Loosen the soil a little, so that it may come out easily. Put a hedge round it; see that it is not killed by anything, and there your work stops. You cannot do anything else. The rest is a manifestation from within its own nature. So with the education of a child; a child educates itself.

**You come to hear me, and when you go home, compare what you have learnt, and you will find you have thought out the same thing; I have only given it expression. I can never teach you anything: you will**

**have to teach yourself, but I can help you perhaps in giving expression to that thought.**

What can crowds do? The history of the world was made by a few dozens, whom you can count on your fingers, and the rest were a rabble . . . No one who is the least impure will ever become religious. Do not try to cover festering sores with masses of roses. Do you think you can cheat God? None can. Give me a straightforward man or woman; but Lord save me from ghosts, flying angels, and devils. Be common, everyday, nice people.

**A fool indeed is he who, living on the banks of the Ganga, seeks to dig a little well for water. A fool indeed is the man who, living near a mine of diamonds, spends his life in searching for beads of glass.**

# Travelling in America

**V**ivekananda told a journalist after his return that his reasons for going to America were several, but in short he had decided to go west, once he had walked all across India and seen most of it. He had heard about the Parliament of Religions in Chicago and was keen to spread India's message there. The Raja of Khetri arranged for his travel and Vivekananda was accompanied by the Raja's private secretary.

The Raja provided him with a robe of orange silk, a turban of the same colour, a first-class ticket on a ship called the *S.S. Peninsular* of the Peninsular and Orient Company, and the wherewithal to cover expenses of his stay there. The ship sailed from Bombay on 31 May 1893, reaching America more than a month later.

Chicago was the third largest city of America then, after New York and Philadelphia, and it was located by the shore of Lake Michigan. Its teeming population and modern ways of life must have bewildered, excited and terrified the young visitor from India.

His impressions of America were mixed: of admiration and the occasional disillusionment. Americans had achieved a lot through hard work, friendly cooperation with one another and the application of scientific knowledge. Not too many years before, Chicago had consisted of only a few fishermen's huts, and now it was transformed into a great city.

Vivekananda attracted people's notice. Boys ran after him, fascinated by his orange robe and turban for they were unfamiliar with this kind of attire. The curiosity was not hostile, but he found help in the initial days hard to come by. He had reached too early and the Parliament was scheduled only in September. It was part of the American exposition to celebrate 400 years of the arrival of the Spanish explorer Christopher Columbus in 1492. In a matter of days, Vivekananda found that his money was running out. Things were more expensive than he had imagined. He was advised to go to Boston, a city on the East Coast of the US, that was known to be more cosmopolitan, and it was on the train there that he made the acquaintance of a kind elderly lady who invited him to be her guest. A professor at Harvard, John Henry Wright, wrote the necessary introductions for him to the organizers of the Parliament of Religions in Chicago.

Unfortunately he lost these letters soon after reaching Chicago. He wandered around Chicago's Lake Shore Drive, and sat down, tired and exhausted, by a roadside kerb. A lady at her window noticed him and asked if he had come as a delegate to the Parliament. He was thus invited into the house of Mr and Mrs George Hale and it was the beginning of a lifelong friendship between Vivekananda and the Hale family.

There were 12 other Indian delegates, including Balwant Nagarkar from the Brahmo Samaj and a delegate from the Theosophists. The latter represented the Theosophical Society headquartered in Madras, that believed in universal brotherhood, in a comparative study of the worlds' religions, the Vedantic concepts of an immortal soul and in the Buddhist belief in rebirth and the need to find enlightenment.

As the Parliament began, the delegates rose one by one, and read speeches that they had prepared in advance. Vivekananda realized then he was totally unprepared. He had never before addressed such a big assembly. When he was asked to make his speech, he found himself seized with stage-fright, and he requested the chairman, the Reverend Dr John Henry Barrows, to call on him a little later. This he did a few more times. He admitted later that he was so nervous that his tongue had dried up.

At last he came to the rostrum and Dr. Barrows introduced him. Bowing to the Goddess Saraswati, the Hindu goddess of wisdom and learning, he turned to address his audience. 'Sisters and Brothers of America,' he began.

Instantly, the audience rose to its feet as one and gave him loud applause. They were moved by his warm words of greeting, so very different from the formal, distant tones of the other speakers.

It took a full two minutes before the applause died away, and Vivekananda began his speech by thanking the youngest nation in the world—America in the modern sense had come into being in 1776 after it had declared its independence from the British. He did this on behalf of the most ancient monastic order in the world, the Vedic order of *sanyasis*, of which he was a part. The key note of his address was universal toleration and acceptance. He quoted from the scriptures, revealing their spirit of tolerance, and emphasized that there were different paths all leading to God. In conclusion, he pleaded for an end to sectarianism, bigotry and fanaticism.

During this time, Vivekananda addressed the Parliament about a dozen times more. He also presented a paper on Hinduism that talked of Hindu metaphysics, psychology and theology. In this he touched on the divinity that rested in every individual soul, and its oneness with the Divine Soul; he also spoke of the essential harmony of religions. He taught that the final goal of man was to become divine by realizing the divine within oneself and in others.

In a matter of days, the young, unknown monk of India was transformed into an outstanding figure of the religious world. From obscurity he instantly rose to fame. His life-size portraits soon appeared in the streets of Chicago, with the words 'The Monk Vivekananda' written below and many passers-by and onlookers would stop in curiosity, and some even bow their heads.

He was soon widely sought after, but as he wrote, fame came with a price. Some overzealous but well-meaning friends, especially women, suggested he take elocution lessons, a few others urged him to dress fashionably in order to influence the trendy set, and others censured him for mixing with all sorts of people.

The reports of the Parliament of Religions were published in magazines and newspapers in India. His fellow monks at the Baranagore monastery were not, at first, clear as to who Vivekananda really was. However, he had written to his mother and to some of his fellow monks and then there was no doubt that Vivekananda was the same Narendranath they had once known.

After the meetings of the Parliament of Religions were concluded, Vivekananda was invited by a lecture bureau to tour the United States, and he accepted the offer. He wanted his earnings to be free of any obligation to his wealthy friends and he also wanted to further the various philanthropic and religious causes that he had in mind in India. He thought that he could effectively spread his ideas all over America through a lecture bureau and thus remove from people's minds all false notions regarding the Hindu religion, and Indian history and culture. Soon he was engaged in a whirlwind tour and he travelled to cities on the American east coast and the Mid-West. People soon called him the 'cyclonic Hindu'. He visited, among other places, Iowa, Des Moines, Memphis, Indianapolis, Minneapolis, Detroit, Buffalo, Hartford, Boston, Cambridge, New York, Baltimore and Washington.

But it was not always smooth going. For instance, Vivekananda would not hesitate to criticize anything if he saw it as brutal, inhumane, narrow-minded and ignorant. He would be irritated by petty questions about India. Soon he discovered that the lecture bureau was exploiting him and he did not like its method of publicity. He began to feel that he was being treated like the chief attraction at a circus. He noticed how its prospectus included his portrait, with the inscription proclaiming his many virtues and qualities: 'An Orator by Divine Right; a Model Representative of his Race; a Perfect Master of the English Language; the Sensation of the World's Fair Parliament.' It also described his appearance, how he looked, his height and colour, and even the clothes he wore.

Vivekananda felt disgusted at being treated like an exotic creature in a show and he severed all his relationships with the bureau. He was determined to arrange his own lectures. He now accepted invitations from churches, clubs and private gatherings, and travelled extensively. Sometimes he delivered 12 to 14 or even more lectures a week. People came in large numbers to listen to him, and he interacted with people from all walks of life.

One of his lectures Hinduism before the Brooklyn Ethical Association was enthusiastically received and there was a request for regular lectures. These lectures constituted the beginning of the permanent work in America, which the Swami secretly wished for.

He soon had sincere admirers and devotees among the Americans, who looked after his every comfort, gave him money when he lacked it, and chose to become his disciples and students. He was particularly grateful to several American women, and in his letters back home he praised them highly.

He was curious to learn everything about America. He studied the country's economic policy, industrial organizations, methods of public instruction, and its museums and art galleries, and wrote to his friends and disciples in India enthusiastically about all this.

His lectures made him popular, and he was offered teaching positions at Columbia and Harvard, established American universities, but he knew he had come to do work of a more enduring nature.

Soon after, some hard-up but earnest students rented some unfurnished rooms in a poor section of New York City. He lived in one of these rooms and a room on the second floor of the lodging-house was used for his lectures and classes. Vivekananda sat on the floor and conducted the meetings, while the audience seated themselves around him as best they could, using the marble-topped dresser, the sofa, and even the wash-stand in the corner. The door was left open and those who came in later filled the hall and sat on the stairs.

The lectures, given every morning and several evenings a week, were free. The rent was paid by voluntary subscriptions raised by students, and the deficit was met by Vivekananda himself through the money he earned by his other lectures on India. Soon the meeting-place had to be moved downstairs to occupy an entire floor.

He had spent nearly two years in America and now he was eager to mould the spiritual life of individual students and to train a group that would carry on his work in America in the future. It was with this in mind that he began to instruct several chosen disciples in Jnana Yoga in order to clarify for them the subtle truths of Vedanta. He also taught them methods of Raja Yoga that included the science of self-control, concentration and meditation. He also instructed a select few at Thousand Island Park in New York State.

He met many interesting people. There was Nikola Tesla, the great scientist who specialized in the field of electricity. Professor Tesla was struck by the resemblance between the 'Samkhya' theory and that of modern physics. In its essence, Samkhya, as formulated by the ancient sage Kapila, makes a distinction between matter and energy (called *prakriti* in Sanskrit) and that of the spirit (*purusha*), both of which are constituents of the universe and responsible for bringing it into being.

He also came in contact with the poor and the humble. There were times he was mistaken for an Afro-American, but he did not mind. One day, as he alighted from a train in a town where he was to deliver a lecture, he was given a welcome by the reception committee. The most prominent people of the town had all gathered to welcome him. An Afro-American porter came up to him and said that he had heard how one of his own people had become a great man and so he wanted the privilege of shaking hands with him. Vivekananda shook his hand most warmly without correcting him. This happened in the American South where emancipation would come decades later after the Civil Rights Act assuring essential rights to all American citizens was passed in 1964. Vivekananda was often refused entry to a hotel, a barber shop, or a restaurant, because he looked different. When he related these incidents to a shocked disciple, he was asked why he did not tell people that he was an Indian and a monk. Vivekananda was indignant at this. He would never seek comfort for himself at the expense of another's humiliation.

Vivekananda made two trips to America. He returned to India from his first visit in January 1897. In between this, he also went twice to Europe. He hardly gave himself time to rest or to recuperate from his many travels, for barely a year later, in 1898 he left again to consolidate the work he had begun in America on his first visit. He returned in 1900 and after a short visit to north India, he returned to Belur Math in Calcutta, where he oversaw the work on the monastery and the headquarters of the Ramakrishna Mission. This was where he passed away on 4 July 1902, at the age of thirty-nine.

# What Swami Vivekananda Said

New York is a grand and good place. The New York people have a tenacity of purpose unknown in any other city.

**. . . I have been running all the time between Boston and New York, two great centres of this country, of which Boston may be called the brain and New York, the purse.**

They have got almost a mania for boating and yachting. The yacht is a kind of light vessel which everyone, young and old, who has the means, possesses. They set sail in them every day to the sea, and return home, to eat and drink and dance—while music continues day and night.

**We must travel, we must go to foreign parts. We must see how the engine of society works in other countries, and keep free and open communication with what is going on in the minds of other nations, if we really want to be a nation again. And over and above all, we must cease to tyrannize.**

Nowhere in the world have I come across such 'frogs-in-the-well' as we are. Let anything new come from some foreign country, and America will be the first to accept it.

**America is a grand country. It is a paradise of the poor and women. There is almost no poor in the country, and nowhere else in the world women are so free, so educated, so cultured.**

I can, if I will, live here all my life in the greatest luxury; but I am a *sanyasi*, and 'India, with all thy faults I love thee still'. So I am coming back after some months, and go on sowing the seeds of religion and progress from city to city as I was doing so long, although amongst a people who know not what appreciation and gratefulness are.

**I am ashamed of my own nation when I compare their beggarly, selfish, unappreciative, ignorant ungratefulness with the help, hospitality, sympathy, and respect which the Americans have shown to me, a representative of a foreign religion. Therefore, come out of the country, see others, and compare.**

Last year I came to this country in summer, a wandering preacher of a far distant country, without name, fame, wealth, or learning to recommend me—friendless, helpless, almost in a state of destitution and American women befriended me, gave me shelter and food, took me to their homes and treated me as their own son, their own brother. They stood my friends even when their own priests were trying to persuade them to give up the 'dangerous heathen'—even when day after day their best friends had told them not to stand by this 'unknown foreigner, maybe, of dangerous character'. But they are better judges of character and soul—for it is the pure mirror that catches the reflection.

**Is America then full of only wingless angels in the shape of women? There is good and bad everywhere, true—but a nation is not to be judged by its weaklings called the wicked, as they are only the weeds which lag behind, but by the good, the noble, and the pure who indicate the national life-current to be flowing clear and vigorous.**

Oh, the terrible cold! But these people keep all down through scientific knowledge. Every house has its cellar underground, in which there is a big boiler whence steam is made to course day and night through every room. This keeps all the rooms warm . . .

**The expense I am bound to run into here is awful. The Americans are so rich that they spend money like water, and by forced legislation keep up the price of everything so high that no other nation on earth can approach it . . .**

All those rosy ideas we had before starting have melted, and I have now to fight against impossibilities. A hundred times I had a mind to go out of the country and go back to India. But I am determined, and I have a call from Above; I see no way, but His eyes see. And I must stick to my guns, life or death . . . .

**Just now I am living as the guest of an old lady in a village near Boston. I accidentally made her acquaintance in the railway train, and she invited me to come over and live with her. I have an advantage in living with her, in saving for some time my expenditure of 1 per day, and she has the advantage of inviting her friends over here and showing them a curio from India! And all this must be borne. Starvation, cold, hooting in the streets on account of my quaint dress, these are what I have to fight against.**

The real spiritual man—everywhere—is broad-minded. His love forces him to be so. They to whom religion is a trade are forced to become narrow-minded and mischievous by their very introduction into religion of the competitive, fighting, selfish methods of the world.

**No other nation applies so much machinery in their everyday work as do the people of this**

country. Everything is machine. Then again, they are only one-twentieth of the whole population of the world. Yet they have fully one-sixth of all the wealth of the world.

There is no limit to their wealth and luxuries. Yet everything here is so dear. The wages of labour are the highest in the world; yet the fight between labour and capital is constant.

I went to see the frozen Minnehaha Falls. They are very beautiful. The temperature today is

21 degrees Fahrenheit, but I had been out sleighing and enjoyed it immensely. I am not the least afraid of losing the tips of my ears or nose. The snow scenery here has pleased me more than any other sight in this country. I saw people skating on a frozen lake yesterday.

A railway porter here is better educated than many of your young men and most of your princes. Every American woman has far better education than can be conceived of by the majority of Hindu women. Why cannot we have the same education? We must.

# Travels in Europe and Asia

**T**ravelling was an immense endeavour, even as recently as a hundred years ago. One travelled mainly by ship which took very long and unless one was rich, this could be arduous. The conditions for the general traveller were not always very comfortable. But Vivekananda was inspired to carry the message of India and its spiritual heritage to the west. India was no decaying and colonized nation; instead, efforts had to be made to rejuvenate and regenerate it. Moreover, his was also a journey to learn, discover and promote understanding between regions and religions.

Life on a ship was very different from that of a wandering monk, but he soon adjusted himself to it on his long journey. His orange robe aroused the curiosity of many fellow passengers, who, however, were soon impressed by his serious nature and scholarship. On the high seas, sometimes the weather was calm and other times stormy, and the ship paused at various ports on the way. Vivekananda enjoyed the voyage, devouring eagerly all he saw and writing about it.

In Colombo he visited the monasteries associated with the Hinayana sect of Buddhists. On the way to Singapore he was shown the haunts of the pirates of the Malay region, whose descendants, as he wrote to an Indian friend, had taken to peaceful pursuits, for they could not put up resistance against the mightier battleships of the French, British and the Dutch that now moved in these seas. At the port of Hong Kong, he saw the many junks and dinghies in the waters and wrote an amusing description of life on a moored boat and how a baby strapped to his mother's back slept soundly on as she moved about carrying loads, jumping with agility from one craft to another.

At Canton in South-east China, in a Buddhist monastery, Vivekananda was received with respect as a great saint from India. He saw in China, and later in Japan, many temples with manuscripts written in the ancient Bengali script. This made him realize the extent of India's influence on the world, especially in olden times. It also strengthened his conviction of the spiritual unity of Asia.

In Japan, he travelled to Yokohama, Osaka, Kyoto and Tokyo. Since the 1880s, Japan had begun to modernize itself after centuries of deliberate isolation. He saw its broad streets, the houses built almost like dollhouses, the pine-covered hills, and the gardens that were intricately designed with shrubs, rockeries, small pools, and tiny stone bridges. The innate artistic nature of the Japanese impressed him. On the other hand, the thoroughly organized Japanese army with its impressive armaments made in Japan itself, the expanding navy, the merchant ships, and its factories revealed to him the scientific skill of a newly awakened Asiatic nation. But he was told that the Japanese regarded India as the 'dreamland of everything noble and great.'

He said later he had never seen a more patriotic and artistic race as the Japanese. He talked about the faith of the Japanese in themselves and in their country. He felt India too would become great when it showed the same kind of sincerity and were ready to sacrifice everything for their country.

From Yokohama Vivekananda crossed the Pacific Ocean and arrived in Vancouver, British Columbia on the west coast of Canada. Next, he travelled by train to Chicago, the final destination of his journey.

The largest part of his stay abroad was spent in America, and he travelled to various cities there. It was from America that he made two short visits to Europe. His stay in England was brief, but he wrote insightful pieces on his stay and the people he met.

Though work in setting up his mission and organization in England took some time to get started, but with the help of his British friends, he saw it to fulfilment. 'The Americans are quick, but they are somewhat like straw on fire, ready to be extinguished,' he had said. He admired the English people, their steadiness, thoroughness, loyalty and perseverance to finish any work that they undertook. Vivekananda had protested against the injustices of colonial rule, yet he found nothing to detest in all the people he met. It was during his second visit in London that he met the British officer James Sevier and his wife Charlotte who would be his devoted followers and would later set up the Advaita Ashrama in Almora.

He also travelled by the famous Orient Express through Europe. His tour programme involved travelling from Paris to Vienna, and thereon to Constantinople (now Istanbul); then by steamer to Athens and some cities in Greece, then across the Mediterranean to

Egypt. It was the year of the Paris Exhibition when he reached. The Congress of History of World religions was being held simultaneously. Vivekananda was to address the sessions here as well, and the only Indian scientist who attended was Sir Jagadish Chandra Bose, who worked on the radio and made important investigations regarding life in plants. In Germany, Vivekananda said the Germans were efficient and the pace of mechanization impressed him as well.

He also met celebrated scholars such as Max Müeller and Paul Deussen in Germany, and spoke of the cultural exchanges that had benefited both countries. In Paris, he willingly showed his hosts and their guests the many ways of wearing a turban and then even posed for photos happily. He described the famous theatre actors of the time whom he met in Europe, including Sarah Bernhardt and Mademoiselle Calve.

Vivekananda also spent several weeks in Switzerland in the July of 1896, visiting Geneva, Montreux, Zermatt and Schaffhausen. He also visited the Chateau of Chillon, the glacier of Mer-de-Glace, the valley of Chamounix, the St. Bernard hospice, Lucerne, and mountain masses such as the Rigi. Vivekananda felt exhilarated by his long walks in the Alps. He wanted to scale Mont Blanc, but gave up the idea when told of the difficulty of the ascent. He found that Swiss peasant life and the manners and customs of the people were quite similar to the hill people he had met when travelling in the Himalayas. In Switzerland, he went mountain climbing and glacial crossing.

In a little village at the foot of the Alps, he conceived the idea of founding a monastery in the Himalayas, and one would indeed be set up at Almora, soon after his return.

He went on a tour through Vienna, Turkey, Greece, Egypt, and also spent some time in Jerusalem. He described Constantinople, its mosques and streets at great length.

He made observations about Egypt, some of which appeared in a Bengali magazine. Seeing Aden, from the ship, one could see only vast stretches of sand and it reminded him of the deserts of Rajasthan he had walked across. In between the hills of the desert, he described the fort and at its very top were the soldiers' barracks. From the ship, one could see hotels and shops arranged in the form of a crescent. Beyond the hills, he described the big pits dug into hillsides for accumulation of rainwater. There was a substantial Indian presence in Aden, not just civil and military people but also Parsi shopkeepers and Sindhi merchants.

In the Suez Canal, he wrote a detailed description of sharks in the waters. They kept everyone guessing when they would arrive and a sighting caused great excitement. There is a memorable description he left of the Suez Canal. He was even well aware of its history.

He showed an admirable knowledge of history, and a keen observation of people and their manners. No matter how far he travelled, he was always happy to be home. He often said that the West was the '*karma-bhumi*', the land of action, while India was his '*punya-bhumi*', the land of holiness, where the pure in heart communed with God. The very dust of India was holy to him.

# What Swami Vivekananda Said

Only I do believe the Western people have the peculiarity of trying to force upon others whatever seems good to them, forgetting that what is good for you may not be good for others.

**The West says, 'We minimise evil by conquering it.' India says, 'We destroy evil by suffering, until evil is nothing to us, it becomes positive enjoyment.' Well, both are great ideals. Who knows which will survive in the long run? Who knows which attitude will really most benefit humanity? Who knows which will disarm and conquer animality? Will it be suffering, or doing? In the meantime, let us not try to destroy each other's ideals. We are both intent upon the same work, which is the annihilation of evil. You take up your method; let us take up our method. Let us not destroy the ideal.**

I do not say to the West, 'Take up our method.' Certainly not. The goal is the same, but the methods can never be the same. And so, after hearing about the ideals of India, I hope that you will say in the same breath to India, 'We know, the goal, the ideal, is all right for us both. You follow your own ideal. You follow your method in your own way, and Godspeed to you!'

(*On Japan*) Their country is their religion. The national cry is ***Dai Nippon, Banzai!*** Live long, great Japan! The country before and above everything else. No sacrifice is too great for maintaining the honour and integrity of the country.

The West wants every bit of spirituality through social improvement. The East wants every bit of social power through spirituality.

No one ever landed on English soil with more hatred in his heart for a race than I did for the English, and, on this platform, are present English friends who can bear witness to the fact, but the more I lived among them, saw how the machine is working, the English national life, mixed with them, found where the heartbeat of the nation was, the more I loved them.

# Women's Education

From early boyhood, Vivekananda had learnt a lot from his mother and was deeply influenced by her. He learnt the wisdom that resided in women, and that they were capable of great sacrifice and possessed immense courage. He knew of his grandmother who had brought up her son—his father—after her husband Durgadas Dutta had renounced the world. He had observed his mother's daily routine first-hand and seen how she had borne his father's early death with great fortitude.

Later, the tragic suicide of his younger sister Yogendrabala and his wanderings across India when he saw the poor condition in which most women lived, showed him that a lot remained to be done to alleviate the sufferings of women. They remained tied to customs and oppressive traditions. They were also denied education, despite the efforts of reformers like Ishwar Chandra Vidyasagar, who worked for education of women and widow remarriage. Soon after Vivekananda set up the Ramakrishna Mission, two projects that were especially dear to his heart were the establishment of a Vedic College and a convent for women. The latter was to be started on the bank of the river Ganga. The teachers trained in the convent were to work for the education of Indian women.

Sometimes his addresses would be peppered with references to ancient Indian epics such as the Ramayana and the Mahabharata.

He spoke eloquently about Sita, and held her up not merely as an example for women, but for mankind as a whole. She always made her choices willingly, and also showed great fortitude, believing in herself rather than accepting others' distrust. It is her story in part that makes the epics enduring, he would say. His thoughts on Sita may appear old-fashioned now, but they were not so at the time, and his constant effort was to speak honourably of Indian women, who stayed in the shadows and lived quiet lives but were capable of immense hardships, determination and struggle. He contrasted the power of the west with the fortitude the east was capable of, and Sita was a symbol of this.

His travels abroad revealed the wide gulf between the women of India and those whose acquaintance he made abroad. When he travelled to America, he was helped on several occasions by women. They came to his assistance in particularly trying circumstances. He wrote many letters to his friends and disciples in India, praising their many virtues and qualities. He said in a letter to the Raja of Khetri, that he had come to America, just as a wandering monk, but American women befriended him, gave him shelter and food, and treated him as one of their own.

He was offered the hospitality of her home by a woman he met on the train to Boston. In Chicago, it was Mrs. George Hale who came to his assistance when he had lost the address of the Parliament venue. In Detroit he spent some weeks, first as a guest of Mrs John Bagley, widow of the former Michigan governor. It was here that Christine Greenstidel first heard him speak and she later became, with the name of Sister Christine, a devoted disciple and a collaborator with Sister Nivedita in her work in Calcutta for the educational advancement of Indian women.

He admired the independent spirit of American women, and felt sad at the plight of India's women. He realized that the misery of India was in part due to the fact that its womenfolk were burdened by the rules of tradition and strict caste regulations. Part of the money earned by his lectures was sent to set up a foundation for Hindu widows at Baranagore. He also conceived the idea of calling women teachers from the West to India to help in the regeneration and reawakening of Indian women.

Among his disciples who would work for the cause of women in India were Mary Hale, Sarah Chapman Bull, Josephine McLeod, Christine Greenstidel (later Sister Christine) and of course Margaret Noble, an Irish lady who became his devoted disciple.

Sarah Bull helped finance Jagadish Chandra Bose's efforts in science. But it was Margaret Noble, whom Vivekananda met in London, who would carry forward his vision for women's progress. Her story is tied inextricably with Swami Vivekananda's. Born in Northern Ireland in 1867, she came from a family of priests who were also politically active in the agitation for the freedom of Ireland from Britain. A teacher by vocation, she also studied the educational systems of the Swiss educationist and reformer Johann Heinrich Pestalozzi and his disciple, the German Friedrich Froebel who founded the kindergarten system and understood that children have unique cognitive and analytical abilities. She opened her own school, the Ruskin School, in Wimbledon in 1895. She attended literary salons and was a member of the Sesame Club where she met Bernard Shaw, T.H. Huxley, and other giants of literature and science. She became the secretary of the club, and lectured on subjects like child psychology and the rights of women. It was at the invitation of her art teacher that she first attended one of Vivekananda's lectures.

At first it was difficult for her to accept Vivekananda's views, but his teachings left a deep influence on her. She wrote in 1904 after Vivekananda's death to a friend that if he had not come to London the time he did, her life would have been 'a headless dream'. She resolved to dedicate her life to his work in India. When she expressed to Vivekananda her desire to come to India, he warned her of the fearfully hot climate, and other hardships she would have to face, but she was determined.

She came to India on January 28, 1898, to work with Henrietta Müller for the education of Indian women. In March she joined the monastic order and he was given the name of Nivedita, the 'Dedicated,' by which name she would always be known and looked up to. Sister Nivedita devoted her life to women's education in India. Later, she also espoused the cause of India's political freedom and inspired many of its leaders with her words. She was also associated with Sarada Ma, who was Shri Ramakrishna's wife and was associated with all the activities of the Ramakrishna Mission.

Vivekananda knew they could serve India only if they were aware of its past, its heritage and its problems. Some of his disciples, including Sister Nivedita accompanied Vivekananda on his trip to north India, including Almora and Kashmir. Nivedita later wrote a book on these travels and her association with Vivekananda, including *The Master as I Knew Him* (1910) and *Notes of Some Wanderings with the Swami Vivekananda* (1913). She wrote of Vivekananda's last days and how a piece of his ochre robe drifted towards her from his funeral pyre and she read it as a special sign. She died in Darjeeling in 1911, and her memorial near the town's railway station bears these words, 'Here repose the ashes of Sister Nivedita, who gave her all to India.'

Her legacy lives on. On November 13, 1898, the day of Deepavali, the festival of lights and also the day of the festival of Kali, the Nivedita Girls' School was opened in Calcutta. Sister Nivedita had first gone from door to door, asking for parents to send their daughters to join her school, but hardly anyone agreed. Finally, it was one of Vivekananda's disciples who volunteered to send his daughters to this new school, and it was all at Vivekananda's behest. The school opened at Bagbazar in Calcutta and it is now known as the Ramakrishna Sarada Mission Sister Nivedita School.

Vivekananda gave her complete freedom in how she ran and managed it. He believed that the society would not develop unless women too were educated. He did not want them to be meek but fearless and spirited and ever questioning. True freedom would come when both men and women were free, for they were like the two wings of a bird.

# What Swami Vivekananda Said

There is no chance for the welfare of the world unless the condition of women is improved. It is not possible for a bird to fly on only one wing.

**They want to know everything, and their women— they are the most advanced in the world. The average American woman is far more cultivated than the average American man.**

This is my summing up: Asia laid the germs of civilization, Europe developed man, and America is developing the woman and the masses. It is the paradise of the woman and the labourer. Now contrast the American masses and women with ours, and you get the idea at once.

**Liberty is the first condition of growth. It is wrong, a thousand times wrong, if any of you dares to say, 'I will work out the salvation of this woman or child.'**

Nowhere on earth have women so many privileges as in America. They are slowly taking everything into their hands; and, strange to say, the number of cultured women is much greater than that of cultured men.

(*On American women*) **Many girls of this country earn their living. Nobody depends upon others. Even millionaires' sons earn their living; but they marry and have separate establishments of their own.**

I have seen thousands of women here whose hearts are as pure and stainless as snow. Oh, how free they are! It is they who control social and civic duties Schools and colleges are full of women, and in our country women cannot be safely allowed to walk in the streets!

**Woman has suffered for eons, and that has given her infinite patience and infinite perseverance.**

Women will work out their destinies—much better, too, than men can ever do for them. All the mischief to women has come because men undertook to shape the destiny of women.

**The natural ambition of woman is through marriage to climb up, leaning upon a man; but those days are gone. You shall be great without the help of any man, just as you are.**

Nowhere in the world are women like those of this country. How pure, independent, self-relying, and kind-hearted! It is the women who are the life and soul of this country. All learning and culture are centred in them.

**Women . . . must go forward or become idiots and soulless tools in the hands of their tyrannical lords.**

It is very difficult to understand why in this country so much difference is made between men and women, whereas the Vedanta declares that one and the same conscious Self is present in all beings. You always criticize women, but say what have you done for their uplift?

**There is no hope for that family or country where there is no estimation of women, where they live in sadness. For this reason, they have to be raised first.**

I am asked again and again, what I think of the widow problem and what I think of the woman question. Let me answer once for all—am I a widow that you ask me that nonsense? Am I a woman that you ask me that question again and again? Who are you to solve women's problems? Are you the Lord God that you should rule over every widow and every woman? Hands off! They will solve their own problems.

# Stories from Swami Vivekananda

**H**ere are a few stories Vivekananda told as part of his teachings, to explain Indian philosophy and culture to those in the west.

## Why We Disagree

Once upon a time in India, representatives of different religions came to a violent and bitter disagreement. One said that the only God that could ever be was Shiva, while another disagreed, insisting that the only God was Vishnu, and it just went on as others piped in. It seemed their quarrel would never be resolved.

A sage was passing by and the men called him over, hoping he would mediate in the matter. The wise sage willingly agreed. He turned to the first man, and asked him if he had seen Shiva and if he was acquainted with him in any way. The man had no reply. The sage then turned to the worshipper of Vishnu and put to him the same question. When he had asked the same question to everyone, he found out that no one really knew anything of God. The sage said that was the reason they were fighting among themselves, for had they really known, they would not have argued. He gave them the example of a jar, which when being filled with water, made a noise, but when it was full, there was little or no sound of water. True knowledge and wisdom left little space for argument.

For men like those who were arguing about the superiority of one god over another, religion was only a mass of frothy words, only what was written and found in books. Every man who thought he knew something, hurried to write a big book, to make it as massive as possible, stealing his materials from every book he could lay his hands upon, without acknowledging what he owed to scholars before him. Then he launched this book upon the world, adding to the chaos already existing there.

## Bhakti or Devotion

A disciple once went to his master and said to him, 'Sir, I want religion.' His teacher looked at the young man, and said not a word. He only smiled. The young man, however, came to him every day, and insisted that all he wanted was religion. But the old teacher knew better than the young man.

One day, when it was very hot, he asked the young man to accompany him to the river for a swim. The young man dived in, and the old man followed him and held the young man down under the water by force. Only after he had struggled for a long while under water, the teacher let his disciple go.

As he struggled for breath, he asked the young man what it was he wanted most while underwater. 'A breath of air,' the disciple answered. The teacher answered that he must want God in the same way, with the same desperation and desire, and then one was sure to find God instantly. Without that thirst and desire, one could not get religion, for all that one struggled with the intellect, or books.

## The Beggar

A great king once went to hunt in a forest, and there he happened to meet a sage. The king exchanged some words with him and was deeply impressed with the wise and austere sage. He insisted that the sage accept a present from him. The sage refused, saying he was perfectly happy with his life in the forest. The trees, he said, gave him enough fruit to eat; the clear streams supplied him with all the water he wanted and he slept in the caves. He couldn't really care much for the king's presents.

The king was insistent, and at last the sage agreed to accompany the king back to his palace. In the palace, he saw the most wonderful things, luxuries that he had no idea existed. Soon the king paused and asked the sage for a moment for it was time to say his prayers. The sage watched the king walk to a corner and he heard him pray. The king prayed to God for more children, more wealth, more territory to rule over. The sage sighed and began to walk away.

It was just then the king completed his prayers and was surprised to see the sage walk away. The sage waved him away, saying the king was a beggar himself, and there was nothing he could give to sages like him, who had little wants and fewer desires. He chided the king gently, telling him his love for God was actually a way of bargaining with the Divine. Swami Vivekananda ended this story with the lesson that the first test of love was that it knew and recognized no bargaining. Love was always the giver, and never the taker.

## The story of Jada Bharata

There was a great king named Bharata. In his old age, Bharata abdicated his throne in favour of his son, and retired to the forests close to the Himalayas. Here, with his own hands he built a little cottage, made of bamboo reeds and grass, on the banks of a river. He learnt to survive on roots and wild herbs that he collected, and spent his days in prayer and meditation.

Days, months and years passed. One day, a doe came to drink water at the river nearby as the king, now turned sage, meditated. As the creature bent her head to drink, a lion roared not too far away. The doe was so alarmed that it leapt across the river, determined to make her escape. The king noticed that the doe was soon to give birth as well, and the exhaustion and fright meant she couldn't quite make the leap. She collapsed in a heap in moments and barely having given birth to a young fawn, she died.

The fawn fell into the water and was being swept away by the current, when it caught the king's eyes. The king rose, having rescued the fawn, took it to his cottage, and for days, looked after the little animal with care and attention. He took the fawn under his care, looking after its every need. The fawn thrived under the gentle care of Bharata and grew into a beautiful deer. The king, who had renounced all attachments to power, position and family, now became very devoted to the young deer that he had rescued. As he became fonder of the deer, he found he had less time and will to concentrate on his prayers. When the deer went out to graze in the forest, or if it was late in returning, Bharata would become anxious and fret.

Years passed, the sage grew older and one day he realized his end was near. But he was still worried for the deer. He wondered what would happen to it after his death.

As his soul left his body, in his next birth he was born as a deer. But no *karma* is ever wasted, and all the great and good deeds done by him as a king and sage bore fruit. This deer was a born 'Jatismara', one born with great gifts. He remembered his past birth, though he could not speak. He was instinctively drawn to graze near hermitages.

In its next birth, the deer was now born as the youngest son of a rich Brahmin. And in this life also, he remembered all his past lives, and even in his childhood was determined to renounce the world. The child grew up strong and healthy, but would not speak a word. He lived very quietly, almost as if he was afraid of getting mixed up with worldly affairs. His thoughts were always on the Infinite, and he lived only to balance out his past *karma*. In course of time his father died, and the sons divided the property among themselves; and thinking that the youngest was a good-for-nothing man, they seized his share. They were charitable enough to give him a roof over his head and food to live on. The brothers' wives were harsh towards him, making him do all the household chores and if he was unable to do everything they wanted, they would taunt and abuse him to his face. But he never protested and his face gave away nothing.

When he was greatly troubled, he would just walk out of the house and sit under a tree, for hours until their anger had died away. One day, one of his sisters-in-law treated him with more unkindness than before, and the young man once again walked out of the house, and sat down under the tree in the way he usually did.

Now it so happened that the king of the country was passing by, seated in a palanquin borne by his bearers. One of the bearers had unexpectedly hurt himself and the king's attendants were looking for someone to replace him. They came upon the young man seated under a tree; and seeing that he was youthful and strong, they asked him if he would take the place of the sick man in carrying the king's palanquin. But the young man did not reply. However, the king's attendants led him away and squarely placed one end of the palanquin's poles on his shoulders.

Without speaking a word, the man went on. But the king realized that the palanquin was not being evenly carried, and that he was experiencing a bumpy ride. Looking out, he advised the new bearer to take some rest if his shoulders were hurting him. It was then that the young man placed his end of the pole down and spoke for the first time.

He said that the body was nothing but a mass of flesh, and it felt no pain or injury. He did not feel weak or tired in the least, the young man went on, but he did not wish to trample on the poor worms crawling on the road, and it was because he was trying so hard to avoid them that the palanquin moved unevenly. He went on to speak eloquently on the nature of the soul, a subject that constituted the highest knowledge.

The king, profoundly impressed, alighted from his palanquin and fell at the young man's feet, begging his forgiveness. The young man blessed him and left. He then resumed the tenor of his previous life. When he died, he was freed forever from the bondage of birth.

## The Frog in the Well

A frog lived in a well. It had lived there for a long time. It was born there and brought up there, and yet was a small frog. Of course, the evolutionists were not there then to tell us whether the frog lost its eyes or not, but, for our story's sake, we must take it for granted that it had its eyes, and that it every day cleansed the water of all the worms and germs that lived in it with an energy that would do credit to our modern bacteriologists. In this way it went on and became sleek and fat. Well, one day another frog that lived in the sea came and fell into the well.

'Where are you from?'

'I am from the sea.'

'The sea! How big is that? Is it as big as my well?' And he took a leap from one side of the well to the other.

'My friend,' said the frog of the sea, 'how do you compare the sea with your little well?'

Then the frog took another leap and asked, 'Is your sea so big?'

'What nonsense you speak, to compare the sea with your well!'

'Well, then,' said the frog of the well, 'nothing can be bigger than my well; there can be nothing bigger than this; this fellow is a liar, so turn him out. '

That has been the difficulty all the while.

I am a Hindu. I am sitting in my own little well and thinking that the whole world is my little well. The Christian sits in his little well and thinks the whole world is his well. The Mohammedan sits in his little well and thinks that is the whole world. I have to thank you of America for the great attempt you are making to break down the barriers of this little world of ours, and hope that, in the future, the Lord will help you to accomplish your purpose.

## The Greatest Sacrifice

After the battle of Kurukshetra, the five Pandava brothers performed a great sacrifice and made large gifts to the poor.

But, after the ceremony, there came a little mongoose, half of whose body was golden, and the other half brown, and he began to roll on the floor of the sacrificial hall. He said to those around, 'You are all liars; this is no sacrifice.

'What!' they exclaimed, 'You say this is no sacrifice; do you not know how money and jewels were poured out to the poor and everyone became rich and happy? This was the most wonderful sacrifice any man every performed.'

But the mongoose said, 'There was once a little village, and there dwelt a poor Brahmin with his wife, his son, and his son's wife. They were very poor and lived on small gifts made to them for preaching and teaching. A famine swept the land for three years, and the poor Brahmin suffered more than ever. At last when the family had starved for days, the father brought home a little barley flour, which he had been fortunate enough to obtain, and he divided it into four parts, one for each member of the family. They prepared it for their meal, and just as they were about to eat, there was a knock at the door. The father opened it, and there stood a guest.

The poor Brahmin, knowing he could not turn away a guest, said, 'Come in, sir; you are welcome.' He set before the guest his own portion of the food, which the guest quickly ate and said, 'Oh, sir, I have been starving for ten days, and this little bit has but increased my hunger.'

Then the wife said to her husband, 'Give him my share,' but the husband said no.

The wife insisted, saying, 'Here is a poor man, and it is our duty as householders to see that he is fed, and it is my duty as a wife to give him my portion, seeing that you have no more to offer him.'

Then she gave her share to the guest, which he ate, and said he was still burning with hunger. So the son said, 'Take my portion too; it is the duty of a son to help his father fulfil his obligations.' The guest ate that, but remained unsatisfied; so the son's wife gave him her portion also. That was sufficient, and the guest departed, blessing them.

That night those four people died of starvation. A few granules of that flour had fallen on the floor; and when I rolled my body on them, half of it became golden, as you see. Since then I have been travelling all over the world, hoping to find another sacrifice like that, but nowhere have I found one; nowhere else has the other half of my body been turned into gold. That is why I say this is no sacrifice.'

## The Dog's Curly Tail

There was a poor man who wanted some money. He had heard that if he could get hold of a ghost, he could command him to bring money or anything else he liked, so he was very anxious find a ghost. He went about searching for a man who could give him a ghost. At last, he found a sage with great powers, and sought his help. The sage asked him what he would do with a ghost.

'I want a ghost to work for me,' replied the man. 'Teach me how to get hold of one, sir; I desire it very much.'

But the sage said, 'Don't worry about this; go home.'

The next day the man went again to the sage and began to weep and pray, 'Give me a ghost; I must have a ghost, sir, to help me.'

The sage was disgusted, and said, 'Take this charm, repeat this magic word, and a ghost will come, and whatever you ask of him he will do. But beware; they are terrible beings, and must be kept continually busy. If you fail to give him work, he will take your life.'

The man replied, 'That is easy; I can give him work to last his life.'

Then he went to a forest, and after he had repeated the magic word several times, a huge ghost appeared before him, and said, 'I am a ghost. I have been conquered by your magic; but you must keep me constantly employed. The moment you fail to give me work, I will kill you.'

The man said, 'Build me a palace,' and the ghost said, 'It is done; the palace is built.'

'Bring me money,' said the man.

'Here is your money,' said the ghost.

'Cut this forest down, and build a city in its place.'

'That is done,' said the ghost, 'anything else?'

Now the man began to be frightened and thought he could give him nothing more to do; the ghost could do everything in a trice. The ghost said, 'Give me something to do or I will eat you up.'

The poor man could find no further occupation for him, and was petrified. So he ran and ran and at last reached the sage, and said, 'Oh, sir, protect my life!'

The sage asked him what the matter was, and the man replied, 'I have nothing to give the ghost to do. Everything I tell him to do he does in a moment, and he threatens to eat me up if I do not give him work.'

Just then the ghost arrived, saying, 'I'm going to devour you' and he would have swallowed the man. But the man began to shake, and begged the sage to save his life.

The sage said, 'I will find you a way out. Look at that dog with a curly tail. Draw your sword quickly, cut the tail off and give it to the ghost to straighten out.'

The man cut off the dog's tail and gave it to the ghost, saying, 'Straighten that out for me.' The ghost took it and slowly and carefully straightened it out, but as soon as he let it go, it instantly curled up again. Once more he laboriously straightened it out, only to find it again curled up as soon as he attempted to let go of it. Again he patiently straightened it out, but as soon as he left it, it curled up again. So he went on for days and days, until he was exhausted and said, 'I was never in such trouble before in my life. I am a veteran ghost, but never before was I in such trouble.' Then he told the man, 'I will make a compromise with you; you let me off and I will let you keep all I have given you and will promise not to harm you.'

The man was much pleased, and accepted the offer gladly.

# Swami Vivekananda:
# A Timeline

| | |
|---|---|
| **1863** | Born on 12 January, Monday, in Calcutta, to Vishwanath Dutta, a lawyer, and Bhuvaneshwari Devi, a pious lady. He was named Narendranath. |
| **1869** | Aged six, Narendranath started his education at a local *pathshala*. |
| **1871** | Enrolled in Pandit Vidyasagar's school, the Metropolitan Institute, in the second standard. |
| **1877** | At thirteen, he accompanied his father and family to Raipur in the Central Provinces. |
| **1879** | He returned to Calcutta and joined the same school. He passed the Entrance examination (Matriculation), performing very well academically. |
| **1880** | He joined Presidency College for his Bachelor of Arts degree. |
| **1881** | He moved to Scottish Church College and passed the Inter examination from here. He continued his BA studies in same institution. * He met Shri Ramakrishna Paramahamsa for the first time in November in Calcutta, at the house of Surendranath Mitra. It was a function in which he sang, and impressed Shri Ramakrishna very much. |
| **1881** | In December, he met Shri Ramakrishna |

Paramahamsa, when he went to Dakshineswar with a friend. He asked Shri Ramakrishna if he had seen God, and received the famous answer: 'Yes.'

**1882–83** He continued to meet Shri Ramakrishna on several occasions. Narendranath soon became his favourite disciple.

**1884** In January, he passed his BA examination from Scottish Church college, with philosophy and logic as his subjects.

**1884** On 25 February, his father died and the family faced immense hardships. He began looking for a job, though he continued going to Dakshineswar.

**1885** In April, Shri Ramakrishna took ill. First symptoms started in December the year before. * In June, Shri Ramakrishna was moved to Shyampukur in Calcutta to be treated for an ailment by a noted doctor. All his disciples gathered there to serve him, as did Naren. * On 11 December, Shri Ramakrishna was moved to a garden house at Cossipore. Naren was there too with his other disciples, but he was also studying for his law examinations.

**1886** On 1 January, Shri Ramakrishna blessed everybody in a special ceremony. * On 4 January, Naren gave up his law studies and stayed almost entirely with his teacher in Cossipore. * Later that year, Shri Ramakrishna anointed his disciples and distributed saffron robes to them. On 15 August, he passed away. A month later, the monks took up a new residence at a small monastery they established in Baranagore. They lived in dire poverty.

**1886–1888** Narendranath stayed mostly in Baranagore except for short journeys to nearby places. He lived with his fellow monks in penury, and they read, learnt and meditated together.

**1888** First journeys with his other companion monks. He made different short trips to Varanasi, Ayodhya, Lucknow, Agra and Vrindavan.

**1889** He travelled to Allahabad and from there went to Ghazipur.

**1890** In Ghazipur he met Pavhari Baba; stayed for three months, left in April to head to Varanasi. * He left Baranagore for a longer duration this time and did not return for seven years.

**1891** He travelled from Meerut to Delhi alone, preparing to be on his own, but in Delhi was met by other monks, and was annoyed at being disturbed.

**1891–1892** He journeyed completely alone as wandering monk. He met people who would later support him in his endeavours such as the Raja of Khetri and the Raja of Ramnad. He walked most of the way even meditating at the rock (which today bears his name) at the southern end of India.

**1893** He left Bombay for Chicago on 31 May 1893. * Landed in Chicago on 30 July, found that the Parliament was scheduled only in September. He headed to Boston, finds friends, delivered a few lectures, and returned to

Chicago in time for the opening. On 11 September, at the opening session of Parliament of Religions, Vivekananda too addressed the delegates.

**1894** Spent in delivering lectures throughout America.

**1895** First taught from February to June. He explained the Upanishads, taught Jnana and Raja Yoga. * June to July, he lived in Thousand Island Park in New York State with a select group of disciples; August and December, he travelled to England. * In December, he conducted private classes on Karma Yoga in New York.

**1896** February—private classes on Bhakti Yoga. He delivered lectures all over America again. He began the Vedanta society in New York. He was offered the chair of Oriental philosophy at Harvard University and also the chair of Sanskrit at Columbia University, and declined both. * In April, he left America for England again and stayed there till July. He would meet people like Max Müeller and also Margaret Noble, who would later be Sister Nivedita. * In July, he left for Switzerland. Then moved through Germany to Kiel to meet Professor Deussen. * In October, he returned to England and stayed there till 16 December. * He made a short journey through Italy—where he saw the Vatican in Rome and travelled to Milan where he saw Leonardo da Vinci's famous paintings. Then he boarded a ship back to India.

**1897** On 15 January, he arrived in Colombo where he received a warm welcome. * On 26 January, he arrived in India at Pamban, then was invited by the

Raja of Ramnad to Rameswaram. He gave several lectures. On 6 February, he was given a great reception in Madras, and also attended several meetings. Then finally he headed to Calcutta by sea on 15 February. * On 19 February, he returned to the Math after 7 years. * May 1: Ramakrishna Mission was formed in Calcutta. * He went to recuperate in Almora. * Relief work undertaken by the monks of the mission as a famine broke out. Vivekananda travelled through the country spreading his message.

**1898** He and his missionaries worked for plague victims in Calcutta. * Margaret Noble arrived in January. * He took some of his disciples on a pilgrimage, through Punjab and Lahore, and to Kashmir in July. * In December, returned to Belur where the new *math* was being built and was consecrated on 9 December.

**1899** * On 2 January, the Ramakrishna Mission opened in a new building in Belur. * He set off on his second trip to the west, and this time travelled through Naples in Italy and Marseilles in France before he arrived in London on 31 July. * On 16 August, left for New York. Stayed for a year in USA, mostly in California. * He set up many Vedantic centres in the USA, in San Francisco, Oakland and Alameda. Gave lectures. His fellow monk Turiyananda continued his work in Mont Clair near New York and in Santa Clara.

**1900** On 20 July, he left for France and arrived on 1 August. He stayed there till October, and attended the Congress of the History of Religions. Left France in October, and toured Vienna and Constantinople, Austria, Greece and Egypt. * Sailed home from Egypt, arrived in early December.

1901      On 3 January, travelled to the ashram in Almora. * Left Almora on 18 Jan, and returned to Belur Math. * In summer, went on a pilgrimage to Dacca (now Dhaka) and Shillong with his mother.

1902      He travelled with a Japanese monk Okakura to Bodh Gaya and Varanasi. * In February, a grand festival to mark Shri Ramakrishna's birthday was held in Belur Math. * On Friday, 4 July, he passed away. His disciples believed he consciously left his body at the time of enlightenment and attained *mahasamadhi*.

## Swami Vivekananda's Writings

*Published in Vivekananda's lifetime:* Karma Yoga (1896); Raja Yoga (1896); Vedanta Philosophy: An Address before the Graduate Philosophical Society (first published 1896); Lectures from Colombo to Almora (1897); Vedanta Philosophy: Lectures on Jnana Yoga (1902)

*Published posthumously:* Addresses on Bhakti Yoga; Bhakti Yoga; Complete works. Vol 5; The East and the West; Inspired Talks (1909); Narada Bhakti Sutras—translation; Lectures from Colombo to Almora (1904); Para Bhakti or Supreme Devotion; Practical Vedanta; Jnana Yoga; Raja Yoga (1920); Speeches and Writings of Swami Vivekananda: a Comprehensive Collection; Vivekavani (1986)—Telugu; Yoga (1987)—Telugu.

# Bibliography

## Books by Swami Vivekananda, available online

*Karma Yoga* (1896); *Bhakti Yoga* (1896); *Vedanta Philosophy: An Address Before the Graduate Philosophical Society* (First published 1896); *Lectures from Colombo to Almora* (1897); *Bhakti Yoga*; *My Master* (1901); *Vedanta Philosophy: Eight lectures on Karma Yoga. Second Edition* (1901); *Vedanta Philosophy: Lectures on Jnana Yoga* (1902); *Inspired Talks: My Master and Other Writings* (Vol 1 to Vol 9), available on *vivekananda.net*; *Swami Vivekananda on Himself*, Vedanta Press and Bookshop 2007

**Websites:** http://www.ramakrishnavivekananda.info/vivekananda/complete_works.htm;

http://en.wikisource.org/wiki/The_Complete_Works_of_Swami_Vivekananda

## Books on Swami Vivekananda

- Chaturvedi Badrinath: *Swami Vivekananda: the Living Vedanta*, Penguin 2006
- Rajgopal Chattopadhyaya: *Swami Vivekananda in India: A Corrective Biography*, Motilal Banarasidass, 1999
- Sister Nivedita: *The Master as I Saw Him*, Advaita Ashrama, Ninth Edition 1910
- Sister Nivedita: *Notes of some Wanderings with the Swami Vivekananda*
- Swami Nikhilananda: *Vivekananda: A Biography*, Ramakrishna Vivekananda Centre, 1989
- Swami Nikhilananda and Aldous Huxley : *The Gospel of Sri Ramakrishna*, Ramakrishna Vivekananda Centre 1984.
- Sankar: *The Monk as Man: The Unknown Life of Swami Vivekananda*, Penguin 2011
- Victor M. Parachin: *Swami Vivekananda: Essential Writings*, Orbis Books, 2012